Don't Play on
the Trestle

Best Wishes —
John Boroman

Don't Play on the Trestle

A Memoir

John J. Bowman

To order additional copies of this book, contact:
Xlibris Corporation
1-888-795-4274
www.Xlibris.com
Orders@Xlibris.com
85312

CONTENTS

III. The 1940s

IV. The 1950s

V. The 1960s and 1970s

VI. The 1980s, 1990s, and 2000s

Dedication

To my family, to my three angels, and especially to all my former students, who made this book possible.

Old men love to dwell upon their recollections and that, I suppose, is one reason for the many volumes published under that name—recollections of gentlemen who tell us what they please, and amuse us, in their old age, with follies of their youth.

—George Crabbe

What would lead an undistinguished lout such as me to deem it necessary to recount events in his life that have little or no bearing on the lives of others? Call it ego. Call it what you will, but for me it has been as spiritual as a visit to the confessional, a means of exorcizing the demons residing in my addled brain these many decades.

Though not chronologically recounted, the episodes fall within a framework of fifty years beginning in 1931, the year I was orphaned, to the 1990s.

All the happenings and the characters living and dead during that period of time constitute in no small measure my rite of passage.

It was the best of times; it was the worst of times . . .

—Charles Dickens

I have had playmates. I have had companions, in my days of childhood, in my joyful school-days: All, all are gone, the familiar faces.

—Charles Lamb

FOREWORD

One Saturday morning in the late 1990s, I walked into Stroud Tackle to see my friends Bill and Eileen Stroud and John Bowman. Bill and Eileen owned the fly-fishing shop and John, a retired teacher, helped them behind the counter now and then. I had stopped by the shop that day to get some advice for a book I was writing about fishing. Eileen advised me to just go fishing and skip the book. John was more helpful.

With his neatly trimmed, startlingly white beard and aviator glasses, he looked like a healthy Hemingway. He advised me to go deep into Baja California, to the Melling Ranch, where tiny native trout still wait in the shadows, and where life has changed little in a century. In *Don't Play on the Trestle*, John describes this lost place and time—the borderlands of San Diego and Baja—beginning in the 1930s, when that frontier was still free and wild. He tells stories here of people who should not be forgotten.

"You can tell a lot about people by fishing with 'em. Places, too," he told me. "I love to watch people fish; I love to watch fly-fishermen. Especially my son, he's a hell of a caster." He scribbled a phone number on a piece of paper. "You go see Conway. He'll tell you something about fishing." And I did. Conway, now a legendary guide and television-show host, took me fly-fishing for sharks. Strictly catch and release. Out on the water, over the noise of the engine and the pounding of the hull, he shared one of his earliest memories:

"I remember my father, this big man walking into the kitchen with albacore as long as his leg. I'd watch the way he cleaned the fish with authority. I'd sit on the floor and just look at him. We'd go fishing every weekend. He'd get me up when it was still dark. The mornings always smelled like pipe tobacco. I remember his Ford Falcon, and his hat, and his red-checkered Filson jacket, and his boots. I still have those boots. He didn't use them anymore, so I just took them. Up until a few years ago, I used to wear them when I fished. They're in my closet now." He recalled catching a trout, and a childhood fishing baptism. "I went into the water after the fish. Just to play with it, you know. This was the middle of February; it was probably 32 degrees out. I remember him getting into the water and just taking me, you know, and running me up to the car and putting me in the car and taking me home. With the fish of course."

Each of John's grown children—Bernadette, Molly, Eileen and Conway—tell such stories with clarity and care. Here is a man who glows in their presence. He loves them in a way that only someone who has lost both parents at an early age can, someone who has witnessed a tragedy that no four-year old should see. Here lives those moments often, perhaps every day of his life. But through a cosmic account balancing (John would see a Higher Power at work), he has received grace. He understands that every minute of family life is a gift, never to be taken for granted. And with great sweetness, his children and his wise and nurturing wife, Marion, never take John for granted.

I have known John Bowman the family man and fisherman, but I have not known him well as a writer, although I knew he was writing a memoir. Over the years, he shared only a few paragraphs with me. Along the way, I decided he needed a proper writing tool, so I loaned him an old Mac. He hated it with a passion (which he will deny, because he is not only a serious man, but a gentleman) and he finally gave it back. John's family set him up with a computer more to his liking, and his pace picked up.

More years went by. Their patience was rewarded.

John Bowman may look like Hemingway, but he writes like Dickens. Or perhaps the Steinbeck of *Cannery Row* and *Sweet Thursday*.

A few days ago, I sent him this e-mail: "I was up until 1:30 am reading your book. About a third of the way through. Reminds me of Dickens. Which makes me wonder where the dickens the author John Bowman has been, until now. It's not too late to write a fine novel." But let's not get ahead of John. This a memoir in vignettes. To write *Don't Play on the Trestle*, he had the good sense not to make a sweeping narrative. He is not a grandiose man. Rather, he picked out moments, some large, some small, and tells stories of people, some large, some small, who were pivotal in his life, characters as vivid as Doc or Twist. One of them is John Bremner—who not only recognized John's writing potential but set an example as a great teacher. Over the years, we've devoted hours to talking about Father Bremner, whom we shared as a teacher two decades apart.

Some statistics on my friend John: He taught high school for 42 years. After he retired, he taught for six more years. One of his daughters, Molly Bowman-Styles, tells me that he has stayed in touch with over 1,000 one-time students. Someone set up a Facebook page for him, and hundreds of his former students now follow him. She remembers her father's kindness extending far beyond the classroom:

"When my dad saw a young man at football practice wearing tattered cleats, he gave him the pair of cleats he wore as a USD freshman because the young man's family could not afford such a luxury," she says. "Our home was a sanctuary for several young men who encountered trouble at home. One student lived with us for an entire summer!" Many of his former students are among his dearest friends today. "My dad's life was shaped by the kindness of others, mentors he refers to in his book as his 'angels.' In turn, dad has been an angel to countless family members, students and friends. I could not be more blessed by my dad's love, compassion and his uncanny perception of the goodness in people."

That is the John Bowman I know. One of the youngsters he mentored was my younger son, Matthew, whom John refers to as Dr. Droll. In a letter home, relating to another matter, Matthew once wrote, "Love is more important than words, but words help."

That pretty much sums up the life that John achieved.

I recall fishing with John in a shallow arm of Lake Morena in the high desert east of San Diego. We took a break and sat in my van and watched the lake grow darker. I told him I was struck by the fact that so many men who have survived traumatic experiences with their own fathers become good parents. He warmed his hands with his coffee cup. "Raising my kids was not a conscious thing," he said. "I think a lot of it was like fishing with nymphs. Nymphs are artificial flies that imitate the larval stage of insects that live on lake or stream bottoms. You let the nymph drift under the water. You watch the line. You don't usually see the strike but you do anticipate it. It's very subtle. Of course, you must have a tackle box full of all kinds of lures and equipment, but the most important thing is time."

The same metaphor works for writing.

"I had to really make myself be a father—not as an obligation, but because I was privileged to have them," he said. "And I always looked at them as being my conscience. They never went to sleep without my going in and giving them a big hug and kiss and saying good night." So in addition to giving lifelong sustenance to countless students, here is what John Bowman was doing when he might have been writing the great American novel. He was fathering a great American family. And now, finally, you can see the bright rings of his words, moving outward, as if on water at sunset.

Richard Louv, November 2012

15

REFLECTIONS

$\mathscr{I}$ am sitting at this damned word processor, my fourteen-week-old Brittany spaniel threatening to chew to shreds my new UGG boots, thinking of the folks in my life who made my job of fleshing out this body of memories easier. A few mentioned in the work died in the service of their country, while others met tragic premature deaths while still in adolescence. Hard-luck Russell, having survived one horrible accident after another, drowned in an Otay Valley gravel pit. Others shuffled off their mortal coil in early adulthood. Ernie, the Friday to my Crusoe, while still in his sixties, succumbed to a heart attack; similarly, Red, my junior high school shot put rival, suffered the same end. Jim, with whom I duked it out during the school operetta, was paralyzed by a stroke a few years after he'd been discharged from the navy where he had served honorably during World War II. Louis, the Herculean dimwit, following his discharge from the army, married, sired three children, and one night in a drunken stupor took a shotgun and murdered his wife, his three offspring, and himself. Bill's sister, the pianist who broke my thirteen-year-old heart, eventually married and at last report (1954) was living in the district of Columbia. I last saw her brother Bill in 1953, when the two of us were employed by the San Diego Gas and Electric Company; my sister, from whom I had been estranged for years, died a few years ago. My Spanish grandmother died at the age of ninety-eight, while both of her daughters, my aunts, passed away in their early seventies, Mary Alice of a stroke, Eveline of heart failure. Ed "Flash" Johnson died in 2009 in Veterans Hospital, San Diego. California.

Me? I was more fortunate than I should have been allowed to be. I married an Irish American lass from Chicago fifty-four years ago; together we brought four lovely children into the world, all grown now and doing splendidly. I, with help from my spouse and three outstanding men, managed a college education.

I taught high school English and literature for thirty-eight years, managed to retain my sanity, and retired in 1993.

Would I change one scene in my life's scenario? No! I am part and parcel of what God in his universal plan deemed me to be. An innocent, young teacher new to the classroom scene, asked me to explain my success as a husband, father, and teacher. Looking her straight in the eye, I unequivocally replied, "My misspent youth."

I

The Trestle

A Description

Situated one mile from the international border of Tijuana, Mexico, the railroad trestle spanned old Highway 101, a reminder of the failed hopes of John D. Spreckles (1853-1926) to build a railroad from San Diego to the eastern reaches of the United States, a project that never fully reached fruition, doomed from the beginning because of insurmountable topographical conditions. But although today the San Diego and Arizona railroad is little but a memory, to the kids in the small town of San Ysidro, and especially with the guys I considered my buddies, it was a blessing, a place to hide from nagging parents, from witless girls, from tattletale little sisters ("Jackie's been smoking a cigarette"), a place where we could share dirty jokes, where we could fart with impunity, where we could look lasciviously at a purloined copy of *Sunshine and Heath*, a nudist magazine, and drop water balloons on the cars of unsuspecting drivers. But, perhaps, it was more importantly a place where we could remove ourselves from a world we hadn't created. "Don't play on the trestle!" was not merely a parental request; it was an out-and-out warning that if we were caught playing on the trestle, there would be serious repercussions, meaning, in my case, a visit to Grandpa's room and a thrashing meted out by his catcher's glove-sized mitts. It was from these womb-like confines that we all began our rite of passage.

II

The Thirties

THE BUNGALOW: APRIL 1931

$\mathscr{I}$t was during mid-fall that I had occasion to motor into San Diego's South Bay suburbs, the environs of my youth. I was seeking employment as a substitute teacher in the Sweetwater Union School District, a move prompted by the crimp the nation's economy had placed upon the fixed incomes of our household (I had retired from public school teaching in 1993, my wife from civil service in 1994). The siren call of the "good-life retirement" threatened to send us onto the rocks of financial ruin; therefore, I felt compelled to seek supplementary income that would provide us the means of paying for our hedonistic pursuits: ocean trips, vacations to all parts of the globe, and more importantly money with which to put food on the table. It seemed that retirement was not the idyllic life we had envisioned.

Thus, as I motored down the back streets of the community of Chula Vista, I was inexplicably drawn to a side street that seemed strangely familiar. There, like a vision drawn from my memory bank, stood the bungalow, a square, cream-colored stucco building common to Southern California in the 1920s. The sight of the small, unpretentious dwelling triggered myriad images, transporting me back in time to my earliest recollections as a child—my mother, herself barely into womanhood, a beautiful lady whose striking looks reflected her Spanish, Welsh, and Scottish breeding, whose passions at age nineteen had produced me out of wedlock, my stepfather, a violently jealous man, extremely handsome, a brooder, a boozer, a blackjack dealer at Tijuana's Foreign Club, a man who I had never seen dressed in any attire other than a tuxedo, his work-clothes, and my half sister, the spawn of my mother's union with my stepfather, whose looks and demeanor matched that of her father and very little with my mother's. Ours was an unhappy household!

Gazing at the bungalow, my thoughts turned from family to the tragedy that occurred late in an evening in April 1931, a tragedy whose memory has haunted me down through the years, a tragic incident that was to shape my life forever—the night I was orphaned.

My eyes gravitated to the back steps of the bungalow, to my hysterical mother's cries that she had been shot, her satin duster coat flapping, her arms flailing the air as if seeking some unseen handhold that would lift her out of harm's way, my stepfather following closely, pistol in hand, firing shot after shot at her fleeing form, my sister and I running after our parents, screaming, sobbing, sensing something was wrong, but because of our ages, unable to grasp the gravity of situation unfolding before our insensitive eyes.

My mother's lifeless body lay between two of the other bungalows in the compound; my stepfather, as always, was in his tux, his gray fedora still on his head, pistol in hand. Without a word to my sister or to me, he raised the revolver to his temple and fired, fell, his body falling next to my mother's. Taking my sister's tiny hand in mine, I announced to the gawking neighbors that my sister and I would have to stay with them because my parents were not going to be home that evening. And that was that. I was just four and one half years old, but that tragic evening would be forever indelibly etched on my mind.

Now, at the age of eighty-three through the tear-filled eyes that had witnessed the tragedy of seventy-eight years past, the aging bungalow conjured one overpowering thought—Sweet Jesus, I sorely miss my tender, loving mother.

On this tragic night began my journey into adolescence and adulthood.

AUNTS

$\mathcal{T}$he day my grandparents took my sister and me into their home, they turned us over to our two teenage aunts whose responsibility it was to care for us—my grandparents because of their ages feeling not up to the task. My half sister's training and welfare were entrusted to Eveline ("Babe"), while I was placed under the protective wing of Mary Alice ("Kiki"), the older of the two girls, both the younger sisters of my deceased mother. Except for their relationship, the two girls had little in common. Eveline loathed school, was shallow, hedonistic, and in today's parlance would be termed an "airhead;" conversely, Mary Alice, the antithesis of her sibling, was conscientious, an above average student, and possessed good common sense. Both girls, like my mother, had been born in a Southern Pacific Railroad boxcar in the Mexican state of Sonora, Mary Alice in 1910 and Eveline in 1913. They attended Sweetwater High School, Mary Alice a senior, Eveline a junior—sometimes. (She loved to ditch school.)

Despite her failings, Eveline did have some talent. She was a violinist in the high school orchestra, could sing a bit. (She was one of the "Three Little Maids" in the school's production of the "Mikado.") Her singing lessons were soon terminated by her vocal coach who frowned on Eveline's sporadic attendance at the studio and her leanings toward "hot" singing, à la Connie Boswell. Eveline's one true desire in life was to quit school and become a band singer. She proved a poor surrogate for my sis, rarely willing to provide the two-year-old with any form of guidance and certainly never setting the child a good example. Her contribution to Gloria's rearing—buying her candy. She never read to the child, never assisted her in her bedtime prayers, and on those occasions when a soothing word was called for, she was never around.

Where Eveline failed in her responsibilities, Mary Alice more than accepted hers, generously assuming the job entrusted to her. She, at age seventeen, became the mother I had lost. Until she married in 1934, to the son of a bitch who seven years later would screw me out of my wages, she and I were practically inseparable. She read to me, purchased a set of children's classics for me, took me to movies, to high school football games, and on some occasions insisted that her dates take me with them, a move that didn't endear me to the young men in her life. And she was talented—skilled in ballet, able to play the alto sax and the piano, and wrote poetry and short stories. Her plans to pursue a career in the field of medicine were thwarted by that old Scottish-Presbyterian specter in the form of my grandfather who declared that no daughter of his was going to go through life, examining naked bodies, dead or alive.

To both my aunts, my grandfather's stance on things modern was a source of embarrassment. Before being allowed to date a young man, Grandfather first had to take him into the living room and quiz him about his morals, his family's background, and its political affiliation. Of course, the question of intention also came into play. By the time the young man was released from the room, he was usually afraid to even suggest holding hands. But the old man was adamant in his demands, perhaps feeling that had he imposed the same routine on my mother's beaux, she might well have avoided the sexual indiscretion that produced me. Certainly his intentions were noble, but on one particular occasion, he carried his watchdog routine too far, placing in jeopardy the social standing of both my aunts.

Summers in the early 1930s meant spending time at Coronado's Tent City. It meant picnics. It meant swimming and diving at the aquatic park. It meant swimming in the municipal pool. It meant eating lots of peanuts, caramel corn, and cotton candy. At least that's what it meant to me. To my aunts, it meant something entirely different—dances at the Coronado Ballroom located on the boardwalk.

I recall one particular Fourth of July evening. Having spent the day swimming, eating, and just relaxing, my two aunts, in the company of two young men, left the confines of the tent my grandparents had rented for the week and headed for the ballroom. Because the tent was one large room, providing no accommodation for Grandfather's first-degree interrogation of the lads, my aunts were elated, the boys relieved. The girls had been gone about an hour when Grandfather, who had fidgeted around the tent like a man possessed, suddenly announced that he should have talked to the boys, especially the boy sporting the fraternity pin. After stewing in his own juices for a few more minutes, he announced that we, all of us, were going for a stroll on the boardwalk where we could watch the fireworks. Fireworks, hell! We ended up in the spectator section of the ballroom where we sat for the better part of three hours, my grandfather's eyes never leaving my aunts and their dates as they fox-trotted or waltzed around the highly waxed floor. My aunts, who had spotted us almost immediately upon our arrival, made every effort to keep themselves and their dancing partners in the area opposite of where we were seated.

We stayed to the bitter end, until the orchestra "wah-wahed" into the tender strains of "Goodnight Sweetheart," the lyrics sung by a falsetto-voiced boy singer, who doubled on clarinet. We met the girls and their dates outside the ballroom where the old man told them to say goodnight, after which he herded all of us off, leaving the lads forlornly standing, quite chapfallen. We never saw those two swains again. For days following that evening, my aunts avoided my grandfather, seldom exchanging so much as a word with him. It was as close as my grandfather ever came to losing the love and affection of his daughters.

A few years later, I lost my aunt Mary Alice to a cad who managed to slip one over on my grandfather, who by then was in the first stages of a terminal disease. Had the bastard asked for her hand a few years before, the old man would have kicked him in the ass! And the guy wasn't even wearing a frat pin.

I consider myself fortunate to have been tended to by Mary Alice; I never lost my love and admiration for her. Her husband posed quite another story.

BUCK BOWMAN,
INTERPLANETARY BUCKAROO

$\mathcal{O}$ne of the favorite pastimes in our neighborhood was playing cowboys. All the silver screen Western heroes were represented: Tom Mix, Hoot Gibson, Buck Jones, Ken Maynard, and Tim McCoy (John Wayne was making pictures as Sandy, the singing cowboy, but we dismissed him as quickly as we dumped Gene Autry, (the idea of a "two-gun totin' buckaroo riding his ol' paint while strummin' his guitar" sickened us). Each of us had his favorite; mine was Buck Jones perhaps because of his craggy face and stoic attitude. The others were "also-rans," which we allowed Calvin Henry, the class cross-dresser, to imitate, especially Tim McCoy whose clothing seemed tailored by Brook's Brothers, Tom Mix who usually kissed the girl at picture's end, Hoot Gibson who was not merely funny, but who wore chaps resembling two large, fleecy sheep, and Ken Maynard who we figured couldn't be much of a cowboy with a name like "Ken." But despite their weaknesses in dealing with the opposite sex, their dress or given names, they had one thing in common: usually two pearl-handled six-shooters; I had none.

Because of my grandmother's aversion to handguns, she refused to purchase one (or two) pearl-handled beauties for me; therefore, I was either obliged to point my finger at the bad guy or clandestinely carve the semblance of one out of wood, both poor substitutes for the real cap pistol and holster. It got to be embarrassing, having to draw my finger and say, "bang!" While the other guys were riding their imaginary steeds and shooting roll after roll of caps at their adversaries, all I could do was give them the finger or, in some instances, the woodblock.

From the age of five, I had requested six-shooters each Christmas, only to experience disappointment on Christmas morning. No revolvers! I began

---

to think that my grandparents were in cahoots with Santa, that the old folks were paying the old gent to ignore my request. So it went for three years, each year producing the same results, Then, in 1935, the year in which I began questioning Santa's credentials, I once again penned my pleas for some shooting irons, hoping that the fourth time would prove a charm. It did, but I was not quite ready for the results.

My list was succinct: a new bike, size 24, a football, a bag of marbles, a jackknife (for whittling out wood guns in case my request for the authentic thing fell through), and, last but not least, in bold letters (I thought Santa perhaps suffered from myopia), a *Buck Jones six-shooter, complete with belt and holster*. Done! Next day, I dropped it in the mail slot at the local PO and waited three weeks for the results. (Our postmaster made it his policy to see that the parents of the kids sending the letters got the missives.)

Christmas morning dawned, a typical clear and sunny Southern California day. But it wasn't the weather which concerned me; it was what lay under our tree. I figured this was my last chance to get the armament I so yearningly desired, knowing full well that my grandparents were not going to swallow the notion that a ten-year-old still believed that there was a Santa Claus.

I beat a hasty sprint into our living room, besting my sis by five steps. The bike was there, the football, a fielder's glove I hadn't requested, but where in the hell was the box containing my hog leg? My first thought was that Santa had screwed me again. Then my grandmother, a loving smile on her face, handed me a Christmas-wrapped box. Was this it? I could hardly contain myself as I ripped the decorative paper off the container. Standing out in bold relief across the face of the box was printed: *Buck Rogers genuine disintegrator pistol*. I was so damned disappointed that I couldn't feign joy at the sight of this abortion with its front sight resembling a car's hood ornament, its grip a broomstick handle, its breech four tiny windows, the holster resembling that which electricians used to carry their tools—a six-shooter it wasn't. My poor grandmother—I had not the nerve to tell her it wasn't what I had expected. "It's swell, Ma, just what I wanted," I gushed. She just beamed.

All I could figure is that my grandmother had gone to the toy department of some store, announcing in her broken English that her son wanted a pistol like the one used by Buck something or other; the salesman figuring to rid his department of these white elephants on this unsuspecting lady, convinced her that the disintegrator pistol was exactly what she was looking for. I really couldn't blame Grandmother. She didn't know Buck Jones from a jug of wine.

But determined to make the most of a very bad situation, I packed that piece for the better part of the year, the two of us the butt of many a snide remark. While the other guys' hog legs were snapping off cap after cap, my twenty-first century peacemaker was spouting sparks provided by flint and wheel:

"The posse, ten stalwarts, stealthily made their way up the canyon, hands on horses' nostrils, suppressing a whinny or nicker that would alert the horse thieves of the lawmen's approach. At the column's head, was Sheriff Buck Bowman, ever alert, his eyes penetrating the canyon's sunless reaches, the fingers of his right hand fondling the handle of his Buck Rogers disintegrator pistol . . . ."

GET THE LEAD OUT, JOHN!

"My god, dear," exclaimed my wife in horrified tones, "that bump has gotten so big!" "That bump" was in reference to the lump rising just below the thumb on my left hand, the result of my having accidentally shot a BB into it in the spring of 1936. I was nine and had borrowed Bob's Daisy pump air rifle. Not too swift of mind, I had cocked the piece and having done so attempted to screw the tube containing the load of BBs into the rifle. Quite suddenly and painfully, the action had triggered the firing mechanism, sending the copper-coated shot into the soft portion of my hand. Shocked, I quickly dropped the piece, running the two blocks toward our house screaming bloody murder, the dim-witted laughter of my neighborhood chums ringing in my ears. I just knew I was mortally wounded.

My hurtful cries were met by the stoical gaze of my Scottish-German grandfather whose first words did little to relieve the shock or the pain. "How many times have I told you not to play with air rifles?"—no words of comfort or concern, just the same old "I told you so's" I had heard since I had been old enough to understand the spoken word. "Well, I guess we had better go see Dr. Brown," was his response to my sobs. "Dr. Brown?" I was now convinced that I would surely die.

Dr. Brown was the town quack, an MD rumored to have received his medical training via some two-bit mail-order medical school; he was also the town sot. If his doctoring didn't kill you, his breath did. An hour's painful probing of the wound produced nothing more than my anguished cries, Granddad's admonishments to "be a man," and Dr. Brown's puffing and grunting as he attempted to extract the shot from its nesting place in the muscle and fatty tissues of my left hand; about every few minutes, on the premise that "nature was calling," the good doctor would excuse himself, returning in short order smelling like a distillery, his forceps ready to continue his unsuccessful probings into my poor hand. Finally, after an hour of this futile exercise and numerous visits to the "bathroom," he toweled his sweaty brow with his shirt sleeve and authoritatively announced that he was unable to extract the lead, assuring my grandfather that in a few years the shot would work its way out. It didn't!

So sixty-one years later, I found myself in surgery having the damned thing removed by a real doctor and a female at that, which would have amazed my chauvinistic grandfather. She did a wonderful job, her deftness with the scalpel leaving but the slightest scar on my aged paw. The BB? It's in my possession, situated in a transparent vial, a gift from the pathologist, a former student, who ran tests on the fatty tumor that had built up around the shot, which when it entered my hand was copper-coated but is now no more than a misshapen piece of lead, the copper coating having been worn away. The vial sets on my dresser conjuring images good and bad from my past—my beloved grandfather, the sozzled Dr. Brown, and the smart-assed kid who chose to ignore an elder's advice.

Watermelons

$\mathcal{F}$ollowing my training as an air force flexible gunner in the early spring of 1944, I was granted what the military termed a "delay in route," which in effect provided me with thirteen days to report to my next assignment. In theory and practice, a portion of those thirteen days could be used as leave, a chance to return home for a short visit.

Unfortunately, if a GI were from California and his present station was in Maine, he spent the larger part of the thirteen days traveling, leaving little if any time to drop in on the folks. Fortunately for me, I was stationed at Las Vegas Army Air Force Field, which was but a few scant miles by Greyhound bus to my home in San Diego, California; from San Diego to my new post in Northern California, was but a short trip to Oakland on the Daylight Limited, then a shorter jaunt on a bus to San Rafael, the location of Hamilton Field. Two days spent traveling would afford me eleven days at home and a chance to visit family and friends and proudly parade my recently acquired gunner's wings around the old neighborhood. I did, however, plan to visit my old hometown situated fifteen miles south of San Diego; I had left the town in 1941, returning but a few times since leaving, and I longed to visit the environs and friends of my childhood and perhaps disprove Thomas Wolfe's claim that "you can't go home again."

After a few days spent in San Diego with my grandmother and half sister, I borrowed my aunt Mary Alice's car and motored south through National City, Chula Vista, and Otay, arriving one-half hour later in San Ysidro. I was amazed at how small the town seemed, remembering that at one time not too many years past it had been the center of my world. I drove around for perhaps an hour, visiting my childhood haunts: the tiny public library where, as a youngster, I had spent many an afternoon, my nose buried in a history book, the elementary school, its playground changed little, its framed siding sporting still its battleship gray tone, the house in which I lived for ten years, its once beautiful white stucco reduced to a dirty smudge, its spacious lawns and flourishing flower gardens overrun with ugly weeds, the railroad trestle where my friends and I took refuge in times of stress and where we discussed, with little understanding, the more tawdry aspects of life.

Walking the three or four blocks that constituted the town's business district, I dropped in to pay my respects at the candy store, the hardware, the Commercial Market, the dry goods store, the meat market, and the drugstore; I purposely avoided Moody's Market (more on this later).

In need of a haircut, my last stop was the barbershop where the barber, Mr. Alonzo, had shorn hair since the advent of recorded history or so it seemed. The shop had changed little since the days when I was obliged to sit upon a board placed across the chair's arms. The walls were blanketed with pictures of the sport of kings, pictures of horses, jockeys, trainers from the bygone halcyon days of the Tijuana track, wiped out by floodwaters in the early 1920s, and its successor the Agua Caliente Turf Club of the early 1930s. The shop smelled of bay rum, talc, and the rancid pipe tobacco smoked by Mr. Alonzo. He had changed little since I had last seen him: small man, slight of frame, aquiline nose, azure eyes, and a thatch of gray hair topped by a green-billed eyeshade of the type used by card dealers and overworked bookkeepers.

Following the usual exchange of greetings dealing with how much I had grown, my grandmother's health and that of my two aunts, where I was serving in the military, and what had become of so-and-so, I doffed my Ike jacket, hanging it on coat hooks, taking great pains to hang it so that the silver gunner's wings were visible, and I sat myself in the shop's sole barber's chair.

In a few moments, Mr. Alonzo was busy working to smooth out my GI haircut, his scissors' metallic click creating a rhythmic accompaniment to his constant chatter about the past. "Do you remember old man Iguchi," he asked, running his scissors up the back of my neck. "You know, the Jap who farmed in the valley west of town, the farm with the great watermelons he used to peddle at his roadside stand. He was shipped out to Manzinar, remember?" Remember old man Iguchi? You're damned right, I did. His farm produced the sweetest melons, a summertime target for my buddies and me. I related to Mr. Alonzo how we kids would sneak into the watermelon patch each summer, grab a few of the ripest fruit, and haul ass to the sheltering confines of the trestle where we would dig out the melon's heart, depositing the remains on automobiles passing beneath the trestle, then running like hell for home. Certainly I remembered the old guy. Hell, he used to run out of his house shouting in Japanese and firing off his double-barreled shotgun at us—scared the crap out of us! Fortunately, he never hit us. We all supposed because he was Japanese and slant-eyed that his eyesight was poor.

Mr. Alonzo, ceasing his snipping for a moment, began chuckling. "Poor eyesight nothing," he chortled. "Mr. Iguchi was one of the best shooters I've ever known. Great wing shot. I've seen him hit gyrating doves like they were stand-up targets in a shooting gallery. Yes, a great shot."

All I knew was he never hit us, and we were proud to the point of pomposity that we had swiped the melons and had lived to tell about it. Mr. Alonzo was mistaken; old age had dimmed his memory. Then, from the lips of Mr. Alonzo came the awful truth, the ego-denting revelation that destroyed yet another legend spawned in my childhood, the commando-like raids on the patch, the escape under the writhing, yet inaccurate shotgun blasts, the retreat to the trestle, all were pure cow manure. I squirmed uncomfortably in the barber's chair.

Making his way around the chair, brushing the loose hair as he circled, Mr. Alonzo related how my grandfather, a Southerner, felt that boyhood should be filled with boyhood pursuits especially those he himself had experienced in his youth: fishing, frog gigging, regular chores, knife whittling, but Grandpa, although he deplored thievery, was especially enamored of the idea that all small boys should experience the hair-raising moments provided in the stealing of watermelons, gunfire, and all. So he had made a deal with Mr. Iguchi in which the old Japanese gentleman would allow me and my buddies to steal from his patch and he, shotgun blazing, would feign anger while chasing us malefactors off his property, Grandpa agreeing to pay for all the pilfered melons. So it was that I learned sadly that all those sorties into Iguchi's melon patch were completely ersatz, as spurious as National Socialist bread!

But I was quick to forgive the old man his subterfuge; it had been exciting and hair-raising, another stage in my rite of passage.

But I have always wondered what Iguchi was yelling in Japanese. Could it have been "Babe Ruth no can play baseball?"

COMIC BOOK HEIST

$\mathcal{T}$he 1930s ushered in the dime comic book, which in reality was a magazine, not a book. The kids in my neighborhood would have killed for the latest copy of *Famous Funnies*, one of the better monthlies in circulation; we followed the adventurous life of a comical knight named Okie Doaks with fervent devotion. No Gawain or Galahad, Doaks was an easier read than were Tennyson's seekers of the Holy Grail; and he was a lot funnier!

Unfortunately, our fervor for the magazine was more often than not cooled for want of a dime, one-tenth of a dollar, a princely sum to Depression kids, whose fathers, those fortunate enough to have a job, were earning barely enough to keep food on the table and could ill-afford to be handing out dimes for comic books when a dime could purchase a pound of hamburger or a gallon of gasoline for the family bus. There were, however, youngsters who solved the problem by stealing the comic from the magazine stand in old man Moody's grocery store. They were the older boys, many who eventually ended up in prison.

As for me, I had been nurtured on large portions of the seventh and tenth commandments; besides, my grandfather, my legal guardian, was well-heeled, the chief accountant at Tijuana's Foreign Club, held stock in the Agua Caliente racetrack and gambling casino, and drove a brand-new Chrysler Airflow. But Grandfather was a Scot and tight as a crab's ass in ninety fathoms. "Ten cents for a comic! You must think money grows on trees," was grandfather's copyrighted reply to my pleas.

Then came the day when, fed up with bromidic monetary rejection, I determined to take matters into my own hands and to hell with Grandfather's penny-wise edicts. I would don my leather jacket, nonchalantly stroll into Mr. Moody's store, make for the magazine rack, and filch a copy of *Famous Funnies*, placing it inside my jacket, and then casually exit the grocery. There was, however, one slight problem with which, in my addled eight-year-old mind, I hadn't reckoned: Mr. Moody had the eyes of a tree-perched kestrel in search of an unwitting field mouse. I had no more than clandestinely ensconced the magazine inside my outerwear when I froze, a large hand threatening to stop the circulation in my right shoulder. "And where do you think you're going with that magazine?" It was old man Moody, and his tone told me that I was in trouble and, perhaps, headed for the Big House. After all, wasn't this sort of petty theft that started James Gagney on a life of crime that eventually got him "sent up the river," while his boyhood pal, Pat O'Brian, resisted temptation and ended up as pastor of St. Mary's or some such parish?

Mr. Moody requested I hand over the magazine and go home. I thought I was out of the woods as Mr. Moody hadn't threatened to go to the authorities, but more importantly, he never even mentioned my grandfather. With a profound sense of relief, a feeling of extreme joy much like that experienced by the prisoner on death row who receives a last-minute pardon, I fairly floated out the door, convinced I had escaped a session with Grandfather's razor strop.

I took my time going home, stopping to launch a few well-aimed rocks at a cat bent upon wreaking havoc on an unsuspecting mockingbird perched on a picket fence, spewing a few insults at a group of girls jumping rope, and stepping on a defenseless stinkbug as it wriggled through the grass. In the words of a poet we had studied in Miss Kalka's fifth grade class, "God was in his heaven and all was right with the world," at least for the nonce. But change was in store.

Whistling, with cavalier abandon, the tune "The Music Goes Round and Round," a popular nonsensical ditty of the time, I made my way up our home's driveway, abruptly halting as I spied my grandfather standing at the top of the driveway, a contemptuous aura enveloping his entire being, a state I had last encountered the afternoon some weeks past when I had managed to set fire to the one and one-half acres of our back property. Grandfather's scowl made a statement negating his use of verbiage; I knew I was in trouble, the specter of the strop hovering before me like Macbeth's dagger. "Get in the car," he commanded.

Without another word, he backed out of the driveway and headed toward town, eventually pulling curbside at Moody's grocery. "Get out!" he barked, his eyes avoiding all contact with my person. Grabbing me by the arm, he led me into the store, stopping just inside the entrance where he released my arm, positioning my head between his frying-pan-sized mitts, tipping my head upward, affording me an unobstructed look at a large piece of butcher paper tacked over the checkout counter upon which was printed (in bold letters) the following: *JACK BOWMAN IS A THIEF!* Without a word, the old man dragged me back to the car, literally tossing me onto the seat, got behind the wheel and without a word, pointed the vehicle toward home. I could already feel the strop's sting.

I did receive my ten lashes plus a tongue-lashing that inflicted more pain than did the strop. Although I always feigned little affection for my grandfather, the truth was that I loved the old bastard, admiring his looks, his dress, his soft Virginia-tinged accent, his honesty, and truthfulness, but I most admired him because he was a real man, a man whose life reflected more adventure than did any of the fictional heroes I had read. So it was that when he reprimanded me, I was cut to the quick not so much because it hurt me but more because the ass-chewing had been the result of something that I had done to hurt him. And until the day he died, I strove never again to harm him. I was completely devastated when, after a prolonged illness, he died without my ever having told him how sorry I was for all the anguish I had caused him, an oversight I regret to this day.

There was one bright side to the magazine theft: I didn't, as had Jimmy Gagney, end up in the Big House!

MR. CAHILL

He is an Englishman!
For he himself has said it,
And it's greatly to his credit,
That he's an Englishman!

$\mathcal{A}$lmost every boyhood memoir includes mention of a neighborhood eccentric, either a lady or a gentleman, this memoir being no exception.

Mr. Cahill, an English gentleman of about seventy plus years, lived in a two-storied frame house adjacent to my grandparents' home. Rumor held that he had lost his wife and three children to the Spanish influenza epidemic of 1918. But the gossip most appealing to me and my buddies was his participation in the Boer War. An officer in an English cavalry unit, he had suffered wounds in the Transvaal, receiving the Victoria Cross for heroism. To us lads, weaned on a steady diet of Hollywood war movies, that was real heady stuff!

Shod in his ever-present carpet slippers, he stood well over six feet, and even at his advanced stage of life bore the unmistakable bearing of a military man, shoulders back, body erect, his unkempt gray hair seemingly at odds with the comb's teeth, his face craggy, his teeth yellowed from years of drinking tea, and smoking a full-bent billiard briar. The hairs of his bushy gray eyebrows grew in all directions, at times covering his cobalt blue eyes, which on occasion were ringed by the metal frames of the pince-nez clipped to his aquiline nose, under which hung a cascading waterfall mustache.

His attire consisted of an old brown cardigan sweater, sans a button or two, sporting numerous holes made by voracious moths and sparks from his pipe, the sleeves, too short for his long arms, revealing the knitted cuffs of a union suit, his trousers corduroy wales indistinguishable from years of wearing and washing. Occasionally, and perhaps for our benefit, his head sported amazing headgear, amazing because none of us had ever seen the real thing: a fez, a deerstalker cap, or a pith helmet.

But our real attraction lay in his house's living room. Mounted on the walls were four animal heads: a full-manned African lion, a Lyrate-horned gazelle, a spiral-horned eland, and my favorite a beady-eyed, two-horned rhinoceros, all bagged by Mr. Cahill while he was in the queen's service. A leopard's skin, head intact, mouth agape, exposing beautiful fangs, lay at the foot of the old man's aging easy chair.

Positioned above the fireplace's mantle hung three framed pictures—Queen Victoria, King Edward II, and Mr. Cahill attired in regimental uniform—over the photos a crossed scabbard and saber.

Mr. Cahill seemed always without the companionship of adults, the one exception being my grandfather, the two of them often found in our garage tending their crocks of fermenting fig wine or working in their gardens of tomatoes, carrots, string beans, and asparagus. While weeding and watering, they would carry on heated political discussions, my grandfather's vitriolic criticisms of President Herbert Hoover's administration spewing forth like the water from his garden hose, Mr. Cahill singing the praises of George V and the House of Windsor, statements leading to my grandfather's remarks that the Windsors were not even English but German. Despite their differences, they were close friends, each of them having led heroic lives, Mr. Cahill in Africa, Grandfather in the wilds of Sonora, Mexico.

On our infrequent visits to Mr. Cahill's house, my buddies and I were regaled with tales of derring-do, his clipped English accent recounting his military career, his hunting safaris on the Dark Continent, his days as a youth growing up in Lancaster where he played "cricket" and "rugby" while a student in "public" school—three words that confused us until the old guy explained that cricket and rugby were English versions of our baseball and football, and that public school really meant private.

Story sessions concluded, from his oven, Mr. Cahill would extract a large pan of homemade gingerbread. On occasion, he would provide us with coffee highly diluted with milk. But the gingerbread! Pure delight—the old man's pièce de résistance, light and full-bodied, squares of gustatory delight in the mouths of ravenous eight-year olds.

I can't recall our having ever thanked him for his largesse, figuring as most kids do that the old man had nothing better to do than to spend his time catering to us. Then one day, quite unexpectedly, his stories stopped; his oven went cold.

In the early spring of 1934, it dawned on my grandparents that neither of them had seen the old man for almost a week. His garden was in need of attention, weeds threatening to take over his plot; his crock of fig wine makings in need of stirring, his two tabbies noted wandering around on his porch, their milk dishes empty, and my friends and I suffering withdrawal symptoms from lack of gingerbread fixes. Finally, his curiosity getting the better of him, my grandfather, using the key Mr. Cahill kept under the mat of his back stoop, entered the home through the kitchen, climbed the stairs leading to the old man's second-story living quarters, and entering the bathroom, found him lying submerged in his filled bathtub quite dead not merely dead, but four-or-so days dead, the victim of a heart attack as concluded by the coroner's office a few days later.

I can only suppose that the old man was buried somewhere but where I haven't the foggiest notion. No one had come forth to claim his body, there being no Church of England in San Diego. The town deduced that he had been buried in an unmarked plot somewhere within the county. But my incurable romantic self, forever at odds with my pragmatic self, chose a much more honorable end for Mr. Cahill whom I pictured transported back to Great Britain and Westminster Abbey where, laid out in full military dress, his chest bedecked with medals, was accorded a hero's funeral attended by the king himself. Anyway, it seemed a more fitting end to a man I deeply admired.

The house, which remained empty until 1936 when our grade school principal and her two children moved in, became the source of numerous rumors, one being that the old man's ghost haunted the place. The town's resident rummy swore on his mother's grave that one dark night as he was toddling his way home, she spotted Mr. Cahill sitting in his rocker on the front porch puffing on his briar and sipping on a large tumbler of single-malt Scotch, his tale embellished by his claim that the old gent had requested he join him for a "bit of the creature." But as irrational and far-fetched as was this canard, I swore I had experienced the topper. One evening just at twilight, I swore to anyone crazy enough to listen to me that I had sensed the spicy aroma of freshly baked gingerbread wafting across our yard on the evening breeze.

The house lay derelict for two years, paint peeling, shingles rotting, yard chocked with weeds, the vacant living room divested of mounted heads, pictures of the crowned heads, and the elegantly attired Mr. Cahill replaced by yellowing squares where once the pictures had hung—the crossed scabbard and saber merely a large ochreous letter "X." The myriad windows of the two-storied house had fallen victim to well-aimed rocks thrown by irrelevant scallywags, one whom was summarily dealt with by an irate grandfather.

SHAKESPEARE IT WASN'T

Be a little upon your guard: remember, he is an actor.

—Horace Walpole.

Mrs. Pitts, the school's fourth grade teacher, was constantly coming up with ideas she felt would give us, the unwashed and unenlightened students of San Ysidro Elementary, a dose of savoir-faire. One of her favorite ploys was the annual school show, staged at the town's civic center. Mrs. Pitts, who fashioned herself a director the in likes of D. W. Griffith and a choreographer the equal of Busby Berkeley, was, of course, to direct all facets of the show, which would feature the fourth, fifth, and sixth graders. One year, we put on a minstrel show in blackface featuring Messieurs interlocutor, Sambo and Tambo; another year, it was a parade of Mother Goose characters (I was the Jack of Jack and Jill), and in my fourth year in elementary school featured characters from famous novels.

The works, which hardly any of us had read (unless you had Mrs. Corbett as your sixth grade instructor), included *Heidi, Rebecca of Sunnybrook Farm, Tom Sawyer, The Adventures of Robin Hood,* and *Robinson Crusoe.* If we could read passably and memorize, we were given parts that is unless you were cast as one of Heidi's grandfather's goats, in which case all you had to do was bleat. Facades depicting the covers of the books to be featured were constructed, the idea (rather Mrs. Pitts's idea) being that the characters in costume would conceal themselves behind the facades and on cue would step out and recite some silly-assed lines (also from Mrs. Pitts's fertile mind) attributed to the character in the book or reflecting the storyline.

I was cast as Robinson Crusoe, my friend Ernie as Crusoe's man, Friday. Ernie, a very dark-complexioned Mexican, was perfectly cast as Friday; I, on the other hand, would have been better cast had I been assigned the part of one of the goats in the Heidi herd. I was much too chubby to portray an emaciated, shipwrecked Crusoe. But Mrs. Pitts would have her way, and because I had a flair for the dramatic, she thought my acting skills would more than make up for my lack of the physical qualities needed for the role. So into rehearsals we went.

In the meantime, all was preparation. My aunt Mary Alice made me a costume that featured a raggedy shirt, old pants, legs torn to shreds, a rope for a belt, sandals, a Japanese parasol made of bamboo and thin rice paper, and the topper of all, a hat, but not just any old hat. Illustrations of Crusoe always pictured him wearing a cone-shaped headpiece made of some sort of animal fleece or hair. My aunt, a very creative young lady, found the perfect duplicate—the large thick-flannelled strainer my grandfather used to separate sediment from liquid when pouring the makings for fig wine into the crocks for fermentation. Turned point up, it was the perfect Crusoe chapeau.

Ernie, whose folks were dirt poor and unable to provide Friday with costume, was also attired in a costume created out of two moth-eaten wildcat skins we used as throw rugs in our home. My aunt initially had given thought to using a large Kodiak bearskin we had in our living room but thought better of it once she had seen Ernie's sparse frame. The kid would have crumbled under the sheer weight of the bearskin suit.

Opening night found us all standing nervously in the wings, waiting to assume our concealed places behind the book-cover facades. The auditorium was filling up fast with parents, relatives, kid sisters and brothers, and poor neighbors shamed into attending. Mrs. Pitts was her twitty self, flustering around backstage, giving last-minute instructions, cautioning us not to drop lines but apprizing us that in the event we did, there would be a prompter in the wings to assist us. I kept worrying that the paper mache parrot affixed to my shoulder would take a nosedive or that in coming out from behind my facade, I would knock over the damned thing. Ernie in his wildcat attire was a picture of coolness; but of course, all he had to do was run out, grunt a couple of lines, and just stand on stage like a statue.

Peeking through the curtain, I caught a glimpse of the Bowman clan being herded to their seats by the family's patriarch, my grandfather, a rooster herding his flock of hens, in this case my grandmother, two aunts, and my little sister.

Following the tragic death of my mother, my grandfather's eldest and favorite daughter, grandfather, like Prince Hamlet, seemed to have taken leave of all humor. He seemed forever eating wormwood. Of course, his being part Scot as well as a Presbyterian was reason enough for his dour disposition, but my mother's death haunted him. He seldom smiled much less laughed. So there he was, as stoic as ever, drawn to this performance more out of parental duty than the chance that he might be entertained. Change, however, was in the offing!

Mrs. Pitts greeted the audience; the curtain parted, and the play began. Having dispensed with Tom Sawyer and Huck, Robin Hood and Maid Marian, Heidi, her mispronunciation of the word "taste" (It came out "taste es") when describing how her grandfather's cheese and how it affected her gustatory sense, it was time for Crusoe to make his entrance, umbrella and musket (an air rifle) in hand, parrot perched precariously on shoulder.

Following a few lines about the shipwreck, my rafting of supplies to the beach, building my shelter, and my extreme loneliness, I shifted (very smoothly, I might add) into my encounter with the would-be cannibal cuisine, Friday. "And behold, here comes Friday from the pages of my adventure." On cue, Ernie, dressed in the moth-eaten wildcat skins, sauntered out from behind our prop grunting, "Me, Friday, Mistah Cusoe fren." On that note, I lost all semblance of stage presence. I began to laugh convulsively; the more I tried to regain my composure, the more I laughed. All the while Mrs. Pitts, from her station in the wings, was frantically whispering, "Stop it, Jack!" triggering yet another round of loud guffaws.

From the darkened auditorium, I heard my grandfather's unmistakable deep, rich laughter, something I had heard only on rare occasions. The more I laughed, the more my laughter precipitated his outbursts. Our laughing soon had the entire audience in an uproar. Mrs. Pitts, in a fit of pique, ordered us off the stage and into the wings, where she gave me an ass-chewing. "You are a disgrace. And you are mistaken if you think for one minute that the audience was laughing with you. They were laughing at you!" I, of course, didn't care if the laughter was with me or against me. All I knew was my grandfather was laughing; he was happy, a state he had not been in for sometime. My grandmother and my aunts? My grandmother, president of the local women's club, was so mortified she missed her next scheduled meeting; my aunts thought I was cute. My little sister thought I was just showing off.

For my transgression, I was assigned to clean erasers for a week, my budding acting career terminated!

CHICKEN TODAY,
FEATHERS TOMORROW

$\mathcal{I}$n 1934, the newly installed Socialist Party of Lazaro Cardenas, the PRI's elected president, nationalized everything from the street taco vendors to the major oil companies and gave the old "heave-ho" to all foreign enterprise. Cardenas's "Mexico for the Mexicans" sounded good but like his educational reform never reached fruition, the victim of craft and corruption that has been the handmaiden of Mexican politics since Montezuma sold out to Cortez. In the end, the "nationalized" companies were controlled by the upper class, the monies allocated for education skimmed off by crooked administrators, leaving the lower class, as they had found themselves prior to the "social revolution," living under the same squalid and ignorant conditions.

No emergence of a campaign promising "middle class," no sign of a school system guaranteeing education for the masses. The rich remained rich and educated; the poor remained poor and ignorant. Mexico's social "overhaul" reached across the international border, affecting profoundly my family's financial status and contributing, in part, I contend, to my grandfather's premature death. On a more personal level, at the ripe old age of eight, our fall from the heady climes of affluence traumatized me, a kid who had everything, clothes, kid transportation (wagons, bikes, scooters, skates), good food, and, with the exception of cap pistols, all the toys a youngster could desire. But 1934 proved the catalyst that greatly modified my lifestyle, reducing me to being just one of the middle-income kids in our neighborhood; my buddies never let me forget how in the past I had lorded over them my social status. We hadn't been reduced to taking welfare, but our income had decreased appreciatively, our lifestyle altered. No longer was there a private box in the Club House at Agua Caliente, no shopping trips to San Diego's finest stores, no parties at the

Hotel Del Coronado with members of San Diego's social register. Where we had owned three cars, we were reduced to one. How had it happened? One minute we were rolling in dough, the next, my grandparents were struggling to make ends meet.

My family had been tied to the fortunes of my granduncle Wirt G. Bowman and his two partners, James Croften and Baron Long, the triumvirate that had created and bankrolled Agua Caliente, Inc., which included the hotel, the Agua Caliente Turf Club, dog-racing track, gambling casino, golf course, and the famous Foreign Club, an organization in which my grandfather had heavily invested. From 1929 until the Mexican reform movement in 1934, the profits had been staggering. With prohibition in full sway in the United States and horse racing and gambling illegal in California, Tijuana became a mecca for the drinker and gambler, for the beautiful people from Hollywood. Then on mandates from Mexico city all was lost, the Mexican government, in the name of its citizenry, confiscating the entire complex, declaring gambling illegal and all foreign ownership unconstitutional, moves that, accompanied by my grandfather's failing health, quickly and quite suddenly changed my life.

No longer was I the neighborhood kid with the new football, the one chosen first on pickup game teams. My sister, though without a football, began being chosen before I was; perhaps it was the result of her having been considered a better athlete than I. Older kids on the playground who had once given me their turn at bat during softball games now, my candy supply dwindled to nothing, considered me a nuisance, ignoring me as if I didn't exist. Once a social lion in the younger set, a rich kid whose parents (grand) threw great Halloween and birthday parties, I had been the toast of the girls in school, but with the cessation of the free cake and ice cream, the scabby-kneed femmes began avoiding me. Teachers who had once treated me as someone special, dismissing my bad behavior and poor grades with little more than a tactful scolding (my grandfather besides being wealthy was also on the school board), began treating me much as they treated my classmates; no longer was I requested to read aloud, clean erasers, or run messages to the principal's office. I had become as ordinary as the dirt deposited between the toes of the school's unshod students. But in the words of the bard, "All's well that ends well." But acceptance did not come quickly.

I ate an awful lot of crow during the ensuing months, but as is their wont, the boys in school were quick to forgive, eventually welcoming me into their cliques, candy or no candy. And the teachers, not having completely taken leave of their senses, admitted that I was the kid who could squeeze the last drop of meaning from a poem, had me once again standing before the class making like a poet laureate. Some things, however, remained the same—the hedonistic girls continued to ignore me.

CRAZY RALPH:
"UN HOMBRE MUY LOCO!"

I never knew cowboy Ralph's surname. We kids just referred to him as Crazy Ralph, taking great care when in his presence to omit the "crazy." Ralph, who stood a good six foot six inches in his boots, rode a large-chested dapple-gray gelding that stood about 17.5 hands. Ralph wore a large Stetson, sporting a band of sweat about two inches wide around the base of the crown. He wore those Western shirts, gingham cloth with phony pearl snap buttons at the cuffs, pockets and front. And he always had a figured blue bandanna tied around his neck. He wore faded jeans, held up by wide red suspenders. But the trapping that most interested me was the Smith and Wesson .38 revolver he carried at his side encased in a holster that seemed in jeopardy of falling apart.

Ralph's person emitted an odd odor, a mixture of Duke's Mixture tobacco, snuff, sweat, and horse and cow manure. If he bathed, it must have been in one of the many watering troughs that dotted the cattle feeding lot where he worked as caretaker and drover.

He lived in a run-down house trailer on the lot, and I was one of the few kids in town who had ever seen its interior. What I remember most about his digs were the flies, hundreds of flies, drawn to the lot by the many piles of manure, most of them gravitating into Ralph's one-room chateau—flies on the windows, flies on the walls, flies on the ceiling, flies on his eating table. But Ralph had a surefire method of controlling the flies. Right in the table's center, he placed a mason jar loaded with honey; the flies unable to resist its lure soon found themselves stuck firmly in the yellowish goo.

I enjoyed being in Ralph's company. I treasured the horseshoe nail ring he made for me. I hung on his every word as he recounted his experiences as a United States Marine in France during World War I. He regaled me with stories of his boyhood in Montana—an idyllic life as he recounted it, spent trout fishing, deer and elk hunting, and working on his father's ranch where he learned to rope and shoot a pistol. And to me, a kid who never seemed to have enough to eat, his accounts of the meals served by the working hands had me salivating. It was at Ralph's grimy table that I first tasted cowboy coffee laced with condensed milk and honey sans flies. I liked Ralph.

A loner, Ralph seldom came to town, content he was to remain ensconced in his trailer or riding herd on his cattle in the canyons and flatlands of the Otay Mesa or to the good grass that lay at the base of the San Ysidro Mountains. It was during one of his infrequent visits to our pueblo, (that's about all San Ysidro was in the 1930s) that he acquired his nickname, and, as fate would have it, his reputation as a man not to be messed with.

Well, on this particular day, Ralph astride Old Bugger, his horse, came riding into town for his monthly supply of groceries. Our border town was noted for its packs of feral dogs, animals that plied their way on both sides of the international border, one day basking in the sun on Avenida Revolution, the next chasing cats and domestic dogs in San Ysidro. They were not only unbridled but also unlicensed and a source of annual outbreaks of rabies. Anyway, as Ralph and his trusty steed were slow-gaiting it down one of our side streets, one of the unfortunate curs made the mistake of running out on the street and snapping at Old Bugger's hooves and fetlocks. Ralph coolly cleared his Smith and Wesson .38 from its holster and put a slug into the dog's head, instantly sending the mutt to canine Valhalla. Old Bugger never missing a clip or a clop from his shod hooves, continued on down the street, under the unbelieving gaze of the onlookers standing on the sidewalk.

Mused one old Mexican, "Eso vaquero es un hombre muy loco." Hence, Ralph became known as Crazy Ralph. From that day forward, the dogs in our community gave Ralph a wide berth, the wild as well as the domesticated. It appeared that word of Ralph's distaste for dogs that snapped at his horse had spread quickly through the ranks of dogdom.

JEROME HERMAN DEAN— YOU ARE DIZZY

---

*B*aseball has always held a special place in the lives of American kids, and I was no exception. I collected baseball cards, followed the Big League line scores in the San Diego *Sun*, supported, at least in spirit, my favorite team, the St. Louis "Cardinals," and idolized certain players from both leagues, national and American, my list always topped by Dizzy Dean of the "Cardinals," and the "Iron Horse," Lou Gehrig of the New York "Yankees." I admired Dean for his alleged zaniness as well as his pitching skills and Gehrig for his heroic mold and his powerful bat. I possessed the talents of neither player except perhaps Dean's buffoonery.

Both players endorsed products then on the market in the 1930s, Dean, General Mills products, Gehrig, The American Tobacco Company. Because of my youth, I was unable to purchase Gehrig's endorsements; however, I consumed myriad bowls of cornflakes and Grape Nuts, two of the products Dean swore would make me a better ballplayer. Oh, I hadn't lost my admiration for Gehrig, but I knew full well that my grandparents would frown on my rolling a smoke from a sack of Duke's Mixture, one of the products upon which Larrupin' Lou placed his stamp of approval. Besides, Lou's products, as we would say in today's parlance, offered no perks; whereas, eating vast amounts of Dizzy's oat and corn breakfast food had its rewards. For box tops and a few cents any kid with a desire to play baseball could acquire for a few box tops and a few cents a manual on pitching, purported to have been penned by Ol' Diz himself, (who was one step from being a functional illiterate), a cheaply made copy of a "Cardinals'" cap, (one of my friends wore his in a rainstorm, turning the cap into something resembling a ball of saturated cardboard) or a baseball autographed by Diz himself. The ball is what I desired more than anything, and by gosh, I was going to get one at all costs.

Two box tops and ten cents were all I needed; I had the ten cents, but I was only halfway through a box of Grape Nuts. What to do? I asked my friend Bob, an older kid, what I should do. "Hell, Jack, they never check these things. All they are looking for is the dime. Send the assholes a top and a bottom from the box you have." Rushing home, I ate a late afternoon bowl (small portion) of cereal and the next morning polished off the rest. I had my empty box.

That afternoon I did as Bob suggested, cutting off the top and the bottom of the empty box, filled out the coupon, wrapped my dime in extra paper to keep it from sliding around, got a three-cent stamp from my aunt, addressed the missive, and ran to the post office where I slid it into the "out of town" slot. All I had to do was wait. And wait I did.

Every day after school, I would check our PO box, the better part of four weeks producing the same negligible results. Just as I was giving up hope of ever receiving my ball, I received a letter that was "signed" by Dizzy, the letter thanking me for my support in eating Grape Nuts and urging me to continue the vitamin-enriched cereal. Then came the real reason for the letter. I was informed by Diz that he was sorry, but he would be unable to send me his autographed baseball because I had sent a top and a bottom instead of two tops. There was no mention of my dime.

From that day forward, I washed my hands of Dizzy Dean, the shoeless hillbilly. I prayed that night that he would not win another game as long as he pitched and that he would fall off the pitcher's mound and break his skinny ass. I began giving thought to taking up rolling my own with Lou's makings, my plans aborted when my grandfather caught me with a sack of Duke's Mixture and a book of cigarette papers I had purloined from Bobby Wright's house; however, in the end, I received some satisfaction.

A couple of weeks later in a pickup game in a field across from my house, Fred Bickle, who must have eaten more Grape Nuts that I, proudly produced one of the "official" Dizzy Dean horsehides. After about four good clouts from our bat, the damned thing resembled a large goose egg, its cover coming apart, the cheap stitch job in shreds—so much for Dizzy's official baseball. Fred was so pissed he tossed the damned thing into Mr. Ezparza's hog wallow where an interested and not too choosy pig pushed it around in the muck for a few minutes before rolling on it and burying it in the mud.

Shortly thereafter, I began eating Uncle Ben's Cream of Wheat, lumps, and all; I never did get my dime back!

RUSSELL

One misfortune always carries another on its back.

—Dutch Proverb

Every neighborhood has its tough-luck kid, the dumbshit who seems constantly at risk of either taking a crack across the nose from a shinny hockey stick or getting caught fishing in a posted pond. My street's luckless boob was Russell, a youngster upon whom the gods never smiled. On one particular summer's day, the fickle Fortuna smote him thrice.

Russell's misfortunes began quite early that morning. We were engaged in a routine game of shiny hockey. Thirty minutes into the game, Russell's forehead received a whack from a shinny stick requiring nine stitches at Dr. Brown's office. He returned to the neighborhood, a conquering hero, his forehead resembling that of Boris Karloff's in his Frankenstein monster role. "Hell," Russell boldly related to the gang, "I didn't even flinch when Dr. Brown was sewing." It was but a few minutes after his return from the doctor's office that Russell was back in the fray, bandaged head and all. We all thought Russell the toughest guy we knew or a downright stupid shit. Most of us agreed on the latter. But Russ wasn't finished.

That afternoon, five of us ventured up the canyon to Clay Mountain, which in reality was no more than a small knoll on whose surface we had carved out a slide. Using old Ford Model T and Model A running boards, bent up on one end, we used them as sleds to plunge down the hundred-foot embankment. On his second ride, Russ hit a rock, hurling him and his running-board sled off the course and into a large cluster of cactus. It took two of us the better part of an hour to separate Russell from the prickly stems that had penetrated his overalls to become stuck in his skin, his arms proving a different matter.

Since he was not wearing a shirt, removing the spikes from his arms proved a little easier. While Bobby and I extracted each needle, applying heavy doses of alcohol to each puncture hole, Russell lay back, grinning like a jackass eating thistles. But with the sun in its zenith, Russell's pièce de résistance lay ahead in the darkness of a moonless summer's eve—Tree tag!

One of our delights during our summer vacations was to play in the evening games like kick-the-can, run-sheep-run, hide-and-seek. But by far, our favored recreation was playing tree tag, a game that required that you not touch the ground unless you could swing onto the ground of a neutral area.

My neighborhood was blessed (as we youngsters saw it) with a row of five large pepper trees, standing in a straight line, many of their limbs interwoven with their neighboring tree, creating a network of branches allowing us boy-apes to swing from one tree to the next. Many of the lower limbs were so large we could actually run on them without aid of hands.

The safe or neutral area was the lawn in front of Mr. Moody's house, an area reached by running along a large branch, springing out to catch a smaller and more limber limb hanging over the fence and because of its limberness, providing easy access to the patch of grass; the branch also placed you out of harm's way of a picket fence that fronted the property.

I never attempted to swing onto neutral ground, content to perch myself in the tree's branches; truth be known, I was scared shitless that I would miss the branch, impaling myself upon the fence's pickets. But Russell was fearless. He would tear out upon the large limb, let out a Tarzan-like yell and spring out into space, his two hands gripping the branch that, bending under his weigh, delivered him to safety, where he would stand, hands on hips, laughing his ass off at us meeker souls perched securely in the high branches. The consensus was that Russell was one crazy son of a bitch.

Anyway, that evening following Russell's confrontation with the shinny stick and the cactus, we all got together, deciding to have a night game of tree tag. Russell showed up, limping, bandaged, but unbowed, that shit-eating grin on his face. It was an especially dark night, but we all knew the location of the branches, so the darkness posed no problem. Until!? We heard Russell's ear-splitting jungle yodel, a thud, accompanied by a cry of pain. Scurrying down from the treetops, we found Russell lying on the lawn, writhing in pain, both his hands clutching his groin. "Oh, my balls," he moaned. Looking up, we discovered the absence of the branch that normally protruded from the tree. Russell had indeed leaped into space; unfortunately he didn't have wings. Needless to say, Russell was not smiling. We helped him home, turning him over to his distraught parents. Reflecting on the day's events, I wondered what the morrow would bring to luckless Russell.

Next day, battered but unbowed, Russell showed up, shinny stick in hand. As I've said, he was either the toughest kid in the neighborhood or a real stupid shit. We were to later discover that old man Moody fed up with our landing in his yard had that afternoon sawed off the branch, leading to Russell's introduction to the picket fence.

THE FINGER

$\mathscr{I}$ remember Mrs. Corbett for any number of reasons, but I especially remember her for the index finger of her right hand. With that digit, which seemed two feet in length, she could fairly knock you out of your desk; it was a real stinger and a force to be avoided at all costs. Let her catch you in the act of allowing your eyes to wander to your neighbor's paper during exams, and she would hit you a whack upside the head that would have you seeing stars and trigger tintinnabulation à la Edgar Allan Poe.

An ass-kicking by the school's bully was preferable to a rap on the skull from that elongated appendage, an event I could attest to firsthand, having been on the receiving end of many a wallop for various class infractions. But despite her having used my head as if it were a watermelon being tested for ripeness, Mrs. Corbett for some inexplicable reason liked me. She demonstrated her fondness in the strangest manner, requiring me on occasion to check out, read, and write reports or present her oral reports on the works she had assigned; very bizarre was her practice of assigning me the readings on weekends, which cut into my playtime but which I obediently completed for fear of receiving a cuffing from *the finger!*

And so it went, the two semesters of my sixth grade term "Hey, Bowman, come on out. We're going fishing at the Dairy Mart pond." Not me! Saturdays found me ensconced in my bedroom, my nose stuck in a book reading about the War of the Roses, the Lewis and Clark expedition to the Pacific, or reading the short stories of O. Henry. I was perhaps the only eleven-year-old, short of the nerds on the *Quiz Kids* radio program, who could discuss in some detail the Lancastrians and Yorkists, Meriwether Lewis's reliance on Sacajawea's guidance up the Missouri, or the irony found in O. Henry's "The Gift of the Magi." No baseball for me, nor big Boston marble game, nor Saturday matinee at the Seville Theater, nor mumblety-peg—hell, I couldn't even spend a few more minutes in bed for fear that I wouldn't have enough time to read my assignment, and falling short would incur Mrs. Corbett's wrath, resulting in a crack on the skull.

And all the time I was having trouble coming to grips for the reasoning behind my teacher's demands. I was the class clown, the cut-up, ever ready to take a dare to do something stupid just to get a laugh out of the more timid bastards in my class, ever ready to receive a smarting smack from the finger.

Unlike Sybil Prather, the class kiss-up, and Armando Bravo, a math wiz, I was never considered too swift when it came to studies. Mrs. Corbett, however, must have sensed that somewhere within my crew cut head, there existed an organ capable of thought because she was never at a loss when it came to assigning me a reading project. My relationship with my teacher created a problem of far more import than shattering my dreams of a Major League career. In the eyes of my classmates, I was fast being looked at as a bigger suck-up than Sybil! And so it went, week after week, into the second semester when we sixth graders were required to take an examination administered by the local junior high to determine whether we would advance to grade seven or spend another year in grade six. (In those days, kids were held back if they failed; try it today, and you'd be dragged before the United States Supreme Court.)

The examination, a two-hour brain buster, covered all the subjects we were to have mastered during our sixth year: math, geography, history, literature, English grammar, which included a heavy dose of diagramming and spelling. Of course, it was a foregone conclusion among my classmates that I would flunk the exam, and, having done so, would be spending another year with "the finger." After all, they all knew me as the dumbest kid in the class, the kid who had trouble with math beyond simple subtraction; however, what the smart-asses hadn't taken into consideration were the many hours I had spent tiring my eyeballs on readings concerned with literature, geography, history, and writing all those damned reports that were assiduously graded for spelling, grammar, and structure by Mrs. Corbett. My day in the sun was close at hand, though feeling I had done poorly on the two-hour torture, I failed to realize it.

It was two weeks following the exam that Mrs. Corbett stood in front of the class, her bony hands clutching our returned papers. All eyes were glued on her; I, afraid of the results that were surely reflected on my paper, had eyes for one thing—the finger, knowing full well that having flunked the test, I would soon be on the receiving end of its smarting sting.

Mrs. Corbett, clearing her throat, announced that she was disappointed in the test results; they, the results, tended to support her judgment that most of the class was made up of idle-brained dullards, who spent far too much time pursuing silly games and inane activities rather than using their time to cultivate their minds. She mentioned baseball, marbles, fishing, and kite flying. I gulped; my goose was surely cooked. The girls, led by Sybil Prather, smugly eyeballed their way around the room, zeroing in on every boy as if to imply we had done poorly on the test and that they, the girls, had aced it; feeling I had received the bulk of their haughtiness, I was now more than ever certain that I was doomed. But Mrs. Corbett was not finished. "And you young ladies," she continued, her high-pitched, Eleanor-Roosevelt voice splitting our ears, "spend far too much time jumping rope, playing jacks, gossiping, and offending the boys with your snobbery!" Wow! She had never criticized the girls, always saving her barbs for the boys. I began to respect Mrs. Corbett. But the best was yet to come.

At the outset, the test results contained a familiar ring: "Sybil Prather's 96 percent is the high score. Armando Bravo scored second highest with a 92 percent." My mind was beginning to wander into its usual funk when, through a mental daze, I heard a name with a familiar ring. "Jack Bowman was third highest with a percentage score of 87 percent." A sudden hush fell over the room; I practically fell over. Me, the third highest score in the whole damned class?! The class silence was deafening; disbelief permeated the room. Then, almost if on cue, the girls were tush-tushing their disapproval, while the boys, through puckered lips, made crude kissing sounds.

Not only had I been promoted to grade seven, but more importantly, I avoided another year with "The Finger." But my joy wrought of having been spared another year in grade six was tempered by the thought that I would sorely miss Mrs. Corbett and her tutelage, which had been responsible for my miraculous showing on an exam that was to prove my last scholastic miracle.

Quite tragically, the ensuing years failed to produce a teacher of Mrs. Corbett's ilk, that rarity in education who not only teaches but also inspires her students to reach unimagined heights of learning. Had I been blessed in later years with a Mrs. Corbett and her educated finger, I perhaps would not have terminated my high school education at age seventeen. Although she left this world many years past, I shall be forever indebted to this wonderful individual who managed to tap the learning juices in a dawdling twelve-year-old.

At my retirement party some fifty-eight years later as I sat egotistically bathing in a plethoric outpouring of praise for my thirty-eight years spent as a high school instructor, my mind returned to that sixth grade classroom with its unforgettable odor, redolent of dusty chalkboards, oil and pencil shavings, floor cleaner, oil-coated ink pen tips, musty 78-rpm Victor Red Label classical records. ("Now class, this is the Boston Symphony's recording of Felix Mendelssohn's *A Midsummer's Night's Dream*. Please close your eyes, and, concentrating on the melody, be ready to tell me and your classmates what you envisioned.") (Oh, that Mrs. Mattie Corbett), the dirt and sweat, boys' smells, the scrubbed-clean "talcumy" girls' smells, but most of all the lilac-water fragrance of Mrs. Corbett as she plied up and down the six rows that constituted our classroom, always accompanied by that damned finger.) God, how I wished her there that evening so that I could proclaim to those in attendance, former students, teaching colleagues, family, and friends, that had she not been that special teacher, the one who demanded, inspired, and scared hell out of me, I would not have been sitting there listening to the accolades all which in part were hers to share.

ORVILLE AND WILBUR REVISITED

*I*n our small community, someone was always building or remodeling something: a milking barn (most families owned cows), rabbit hutches (ditto), chicken coops (ditto), or in the case of some of the less enlightened citizenry new outhouses. So it was that there was always a good supply of scrap lumber available to the kids in my neighborhood for fashioning sidewalk scooters, the precursor of today's skateboard, a device constructed of one-roller skate, a two by four, and if you could bag one from the local grocery store, an orange crate nailed in an upright position to the two by four. A joy to the younger crowd, the scooters were a bane to stray dogs, cats, or old ladies who happened to be in the path of the town's hooligans as they raced madly down the local sidewalks.

It was from this ready supply of lumber that Bob, the "genius" behind the ill-fated eight-foot box kite, Charlie, the local librarian's son, and I fashioned our own version of Otto Lilenthal's manned glider, an idea that sprang fully-armed from Bob's fertile mind. He enlisted Charlie's assistance because of Charlie's size and strength. (Charlie, at age fifteen, possessed the anatomy of a college football interior lineman.) He chose me because of my imbecility and my skill as a thief. (You see, the loose lumber was not for the taking but rather it had to be pilfered.) The three of us set about the task of acquiring the necessary materials for the construction of our glider: Scrap lumber for the body, wings, and tail section, sheets for the fabric coverings of body, wings, and tail. (Our parents' linen closets were hit hard). A few boxes of carpet tacks, various screws and nuts, and a gallon of aviation dope, used to tauten the cloth surfaces of airplane wing and tail surfaces, was procured from Bob's aviator uncle. We were ready to begin construction.

Within a month, our engineless aircraft was completed and ready to be transported to a hill with a precipitous cliff that dropped thirty feet to a pile of large boulders. Realizing that to reach the launch site would take some transporting, we had built the craft in sections: body, two sections of wing, to be attached to the fuselage with screws, likewise a tail section affixed in the same manner. Charlie, the strongest of our trio, packed the fuselage, Bob the wing sections, while I, the runt, wrestled with the tail section.

Together, one Saturday morning, we wound our way up the canyon leading to the takeoff point. Once atop the hill, we assembled our creation; we were very soon to learn, much to Bob's despair, that we were not aeronautical engineers. The flight plan was quite simple: Bob was to step into the opening in the fuselage's center, grip the side handles, picking up the glider until it was aligned with his midriff, run at full tilt down the slope, and soar out over the cliff's edge, sailing across the canyon, landing unscathed on the opposite side.

Seemingly a safe and simple plan, Charlie and I trotted to the cliff's edge, awaiting Bob's dash toward the takeoff point. With a howl, Bob began the run of about forty yards. But why were the wings flapping up and down? Hitting the edge of rim of the cliff, Bob and glider, released from earth's bonds, were propelled into thin air. Actually they were but a few feet into space when the wings folded up like two outstretched arms, the craft and Bob plummeting straight down onto the boulders strewn at the cliff's base.

Dumbfounded, Charlie and I raced down to the canyon floor where Bob lay in a heap of wood and bedsheets, his shirt ripped, his right pant leg torn, his leg broken, the fibula protruding from his calf. Abandoning the remains of the fallen bird, Charlie and I managed to get Bob back to his house where we found his mother busy at the kitchen sink. "Bob's got a compound fractured leg!" blurted Charlie.

"Yeah," I chimed in and added, "a compound fracture of his right leg. The bone is sticking out!" Bob's mother, a woman more concerned with her weekly bridge parties than she was with her two children, without so much as a glance at her son's mangled leg, insensibly snorted, "Take him out on the back porch. He's dripping blood all over my clean floor!"

What to do? I suggested we take Bob to my grandfather, who, though always in full possession of his mental faculties, happened to be very fond of Bob. There was, however, one problem: We would be obliged to relate to Grandfather the circumstances that had led to Bob's injury. Oh boy! Once his lecture on the follies of youth ended and Bob had been placed on the passenger's side of Grandfather's DeSoto coupe, the four of us, Charlie and I in the rumble seat, the old man "put the pedal to the metal" and made for Dr. Brown's office. Although finding the good doctor in his cups, he was sober enough to set Bob's leg, place it in a cast, and give him the loan of a crutch.

Bob's dream of soaring, unfettered by the bonds of earth, lay in a crumpled mess at the foot of Clay Mountain where it remained for years, a reminder that grandfathers were more than old men in tattered brown sweaters that smelled of tobacco and sweat, that the young would be wise to listen to their advice, advice born of experience. Acknowledgment of these facts was slow in coming.

Bob and Charlie? Bob became a pilot as soon as he was old enough to take lessons and solo; as an adult, he headed a sheriff's helicopter unit in Southern California. Charlie, following a career as an attorney, became a municipal judge.

THE GREEKS HAD A WORD FOR IT

*B*ig Boston, Little Boston, Fish, Poison, Chase (games) agates, purees, steelies, boulders, dobes, peewees (marbles), upsies, mounds, knuckles down, fudging were the lexicon of springtime madness in my neighborhood. To the uninitiated "marbles"-"migs." No sooner had the ground in our vacant lots shed their mantle of winter's wetness then the clack of glass upon glass resounded from Bull Durham sacks bulging with "migs" of every description. Agates were left to soak a few days in the family's Crisco cans, the theory being that doing so gave the shooter a better chance of sticking inside the large circle of Big Boston, affording the keen-eyed shooter a better chance of cleaning the ring. Marbles were separated into categories: shooters, marbles valued for their feel, their touch between thumb and forefinger, laggers, heavy marbles used in line-lagging that determined shooting rotation in games such as Big and Little Boston, and dates, the throwaways, chipped or imperfect marbles, the pawns, the sacrificial glass vassals, whose worth we cared little for. Then there were the dobies, cheap imitations fashioned from adobe and cheaply purchased in Tijuana, that only the dumbshits in our crowd attempted to pawn off as the real thing.

Of all the neighborhood striplings, I was the most sorry-assed individual to take part in this adolescent rite of springtime. As predictable as the first buds on our family's fruit trees, I was destined to be divested of every marble I had received for my birthday, Christmas and my Saint's Day. Kids who lived on my block began salivating at the prospects of luring me into our initial game, realizing that one game of Big Boston, a game in which each competitor dated up twenty-five or thirty marbles, would enhance their stash, bulging their marble sacks to the bursting point. In a word, I was their patsy. But by the spring of 1935 would prove their undoing!

From pre-smog Los Angeles he came, a fifteen-year-old hunk of masculine pulchritude, a junior version of the Arrow Collar Man, an athlete of great renown at Benjamin Franklin High School in Highland Park, and more importantly, along York Boulevard, a wizard in shooting the glass taw. He was also my cousin, who had come to visit our family during Easter vacation. He hadn't unpacked his suitcase before I was making plans to utilize his educated forefinger and thumb and his deadly eye. Not only did I envision Easter baskets laden with candy eggs and milk chocolate bunnies, but I also visualized coffers heavy with marbles liberated from my unsuspecting neighborhood chums, revenging the many springs I had suffered the humiliation of playing pigeon to not only the boys in our crowd but also a few tomboys as well, including my little sister. It was going to be a very profitable Easter. "Dame Fortune," that fickle bitch, had other plans for me!

By Good Saturday, my cousin had cleaned, gleaned, divested, requisitioned, sucked, drained every last marble from every frigging hooligan living within the boundaries of my block, every last glass orb ensconced in a large General Mills' flour sack, the flawed migs dispatched by slingshot at unsuspecting birds, cats, girls, and a large white mule corralled across the canyon from my street; the crème de la crème, I deposited upon my bed to be counted over and over, my eyes glinting avariciously like Humphrey Bogart's as he stared at his "goods" in the classic film *Treasure of the Sierra Madre*. And like Fred C. Dobbs, I, too, was destined to pay for my greed.

On the Monday after Easter Sunday, my grandfather, at the wheel of the family's De Soto sedan, drove my cousin to the foot of Broadway in San Diego, to the Santa Fe Railroad Depot, where, ticket purchased, my champion boarded the Los Angeles bound express train. Rather than accompanying them to the station, I remained at home, holed up in my room, sorting and re-sorting my newly acquired wealth. But why were the neighborhood kids loitering around in front of our house looking like a mob of eighteenth-century French peasants in search of candidates for a date with Madame Guillotine? Why was I feeling a little like Louis XIV? Tuesday, our first day back in school following Easter vacation, would prove a day of reckoning.

By the end of the school day, my cache had been reduced to zilch! I was cleaned out, left standing forlornly on the lower playground, an empty flour sack drooping at my side, tears welling in my eyes, the source of my humiliation and undoing sniggering and braying as they swaggered toward the upper field occasionally casting an over-the-shoulder sneer in my direction, punctuated by an expletive or two.

Downcast, I made for the playground's lower gate, then, having safely exited and being a safe distance from my antagonists, I boldly raised my right arm to its full length, extended my middle finger, and shouted, "Fuck all you lousy bastards," and took off running home, the "lousy bastards" in hot pursuit! But in my haste to mete out retaliation short of the draconian, I'd forgotten the reasons for my having been saddled with the sobriquet "Lard Ass!" I was the most unathletic boy in school, and to make my situation direr, also the slowest resulting in my being cornered by four young thugs who summarily beat the snot out of me. It wasn't until many years later that I learned the penalty for hubris.

The Greeks had a name for it, and like Achilles, I learned the hard way.

GRANDFATHER

He was a man, take him for all and all,
I shall not look upon his like again.

—William Shakespeare

My grandfather seemed always in search of a remedy for his stomach problems: milk of magnesia, bicarbonate of soda, the fetid water of the natural sulfur spring at Warner's Hot Spring. When my great-grandmother, who also suffered from various stomach problems, aliments, real and imagined, visited us from her home in San Pedro, the two of them were constantly sharing their latest panacea. Grandfather went on diets, eliminated certain foods from his daily fare, drove my grandmother crazy by insisting his food be boiled, sautéed, broiled, or baked. But the real tip-off that he was ill was when he quit requesting gravy with his meals. A Southerner by birth, he had been reared on the premise that no meal was complete unless the meat and potatoes were drowned in meat drippings laced with some flour and water.

For some months my grandfather had been in and out of the hospital, doctors are unable to diagnose the cause of an illness that had manifested itself one night while he and my uncle were having a late evening snack, following their attendance at the prizefight card at San Diego's Coliseum. Since that evening, the members of our household, my sister and I in particular, had adopted a code of silence. We spoke in hushed tones, tiptoed through the house, and, in general, took on the conduct of the cloistered members of a monastery. But despite our precautions, he was admitted to Mercy Hospital for the last time in mid-April. I was never to see him alive again.

I had always considered my grandfather immortal, a giant impervious to illness and death. He was bigger than life, a man whose life from early manhood read like something from the pages of James Fenimore Cooper or Owen Wister. His passing triggered my first concerns about my own mortality: If death came to my bigger-than-life grandfather, what chance did I have to live forever? Granted my parents died a most tragic death when I was but four years of age, but because of my innocence, I was able to commit any thoughts of dying and the tragedy I had witnessed into the recesses of my young mind where they would remain dormant, becoming demons only after I had reached adulthood. My grandfather's death differed.

I was ten years old, and his death became very real and because I had no room left in that portion of my mind that harbored the thoughts of my parents passing, Grandfather's demise left me in a state of funk; I felt betrayed, and though I dearly loved him, I cursed the old bastard for having deserted me when I had great need of him and his guidance. He had, since the death of my parents, been my father, and now I found myself orphaned for a second time. It wasn't fair! After all, Natty Bumpo had met the Grim Reaper when he was almost hundred years old; how dare my grandfather to die at only fifty-six. Given the circumstances of his life, I thought him immortal.

Born in Virginia to a Scots-German father and a Welsh mother, my grandfather's adult life really began when, in 1902, he ventured into the state of Sonora, Mexico, where he remained until 1914 at which time he, his young Spanish spouse and three daughters traveled north to establish residence in Nogalas, Arizona, where he served as deputy sheriff of Santa Cruz County.

While in Mexico, he served as station agent for the Southern Pacific Railroad of Mexico, fought the ferocious Yaqui Indians, beat off attacks from marauding bands of Mexican brigands, with his young wife who set up housekeeping in a boxcar, witnessed the birth of three daughters in that same boxcar, became fluent in the Spanish language, gained the respect of his Mexican employees, (one who eventually became a general in the revolutionary armies) and perhaps more importantly managed to be tolerant with his Catholic Spanish mother-in-law's intolerance toward him.

My grandfather (a Presbyterian), was a man among men, a true hero if ever there was one. And he had, in later years, the leathery look of Walter Huston, in the movie *Treasure of the Sierra Madre*, the soft Virginia accent of Joseph Cotton, and the build of a blacksmith, with ham-sized hands to match. He was, in essence, a paradox, bigoted, yet liberal, outspoken, yet a good listener; stubborn, yet flexible. A dyed-in-the wool Southern Democrat, he voted for FDR in 1931, losing a very close friend who had supported Hoover.

He loved Tom Mix Westerns, vaudeville, Chrysler products, Hart, Schaffner and Marx suits, Amos and Andy, my grandmother and his three daughters, fried chicken, prizefights, Mexicans, and the USC "Trojan" football team; conversely, he openly abhorred Negroes, Jews, Mr. Hoover, my stepfather, my natural father, braggarts, bullies, social posturing, doctors (didn't trust them), household pets, and in a lesser sense me, a constant reminder of his favorite daughter's teen sexual indiscretion.

In 1931, he took on the responsibility of raising his two grandchildren, my sister and me, at age fifty, legally adopting us five years later. He was able, through some connection, to have my birth certificate altered to indicate my grandmother and he as my natural parents, thereby removing the stigma of my illegitimacy.

Perhaps because of his age, or the beginnings of his fatal illness, grandfather was unable to adjust to the invasion of his sanctuary by two mischievous children. We were just a little too much for him, often trying his patience to the breaking point. Then, too, the memory of my mother's tragic and untimely death haunted him for the six remaining years of his life. Oh, he tried. My god, how he tried. But he could not show either of us the affection we so desperately needed. I think that in many ways, he resented us for upsetting his up-to-then very structured life. His efforts at being warm were pure sham; he treated us with indifference, especially me. And I felt it. I recall being on the receiving end of many a spanking at his hands, his huge, ham-sized hands. Granted many were deserved, some not, a few the result of his having believed my lying sister instead of the truthful me. I started believing George Washington was a damned fool; he should have blamed the family gardener for the demise of that cherry tree.

Grandfather's moods wavered between caring father and detached grandparent. I can recall times when he was a fatherly exemplar; for instance, my lifelong love of football stems from my grandfather having taken me to numerous SC games at the Los Angeles Coliseum. We sat ringside at prizefights, after which we retired to Frenchy's restaurant in National City for a late-night snack. But the negative experiences far outweighed the positive; I had come along much too late in his life, and he was either unwilling or unable to be my father. But I dearly loved and respected him. On a rather warm evening for April, we neighborhood kids were playing a noisy game of "Run Sheep Run," when my aunt Eveline pulled me aside and told me that my grandfather had died that morning. I recall losing sensation in my legs, my head swirling seemingly detached from my neck, waves of nausea sweeping through my entire being.

He was gone, and I was in a state of denial for the better part of a week; it was when I was forced to lean into his coffin and kiss his cold, waxen face that I accepted his passing and even then, I half expected him to sit up and give me a good ass-chewing. But he didn't! He was really gone, and in the words of Robert Frost there was "nothing to build on here."

THE WORM TURNS

$\mathcal{N}$ineteen was the age when she gave birth to son, my mother, only a child herself, quickly turned the rearing of her infant son into the hands of my maternal grandparents, and just as quickly left town, supposedly relinquishing all claim to her illegitimate son. And although my grandparents carried still the stigma and shame of their eldest daughter's sexual transgression, they, without hesitation, took me into their home where they planned to raise me as their natural son, a replacement for the boy-child my grandmother had miscarried in 1905 during the third month of her first pregnancy. An easy decision for my grandmother, my entry into the family posed quite a different dilemma for my grandfather, a man schooled from early childhood in the tenets of Calvinism. But my grandfather's deep love for my grandmother proved stronger than did the moral teachings of Presbyterianism, and he, too, after a fashion, took the bastard grandson as his own. My mother? She quickly married, convincing her groom that he was my natural father when, in reality, my real father had left town soon after my mother announced that she was pregnant, catching a fast train north to Canada before my mother's shocking news had cleared her lips, one step ahead of my infuriated grandfather.

Two years later, Mother was back home, laying claim to the infant son she had given my grandparents. It seems that following her marriage, she and her husband, at the time the owner and trainer of three race horses, had traveled to racing meets as far north as Vancouver, Canada, and east to Omaha, Nebraska. At some point during their travels, my mother, seemingly unable to conceive, visited a physician, who announced that she would never again bear children, after which my mother hied herself back to the old homestead and me, who by then was addressing my grandparents as "mu" and "da." She just as quickly, left town, me in tow, to join my stepfather and his stable of platters in a godforsaken tank town in Eastern Washington where a ten-day race meet

---

was in progress. It was shortly after she and my stepfather were united that she became pregnant; nine months later, she gave birth to my half sister, Gloria Josephine, who, until my entry into the military during World War II, became an annoying boil on my bum. So much for the doctor's prognosis!

The only common denominator Gloria Jo and I shared was having been born of the same mother. Our one difference was obvious to even the casual observer: dark complexion, coal-black hair, and almond eyes, my sister was the spitting image of her dad, whose paternal grandmother was part Choctaw Indian; I, on the other hand, with the exception of some Spanish blood, was Anglo-Saxon/Celt, whey-faced, towheaded, and blue-eyed. There were yet other differences not evident while we were in infancy, differences other than the physical, differences that in later years would cause a rift in our sister-brother relationship, a fissure that exists today.

Following my parents' tragic and untimely death in 1931, my sister and I were remanded to the custody of my grandparents; my grandfather was fifty, my grandmother forty-five; perhaps because neither of them had the patience to deal with us, we were summarily turned over to the care of our two teenage aunts.

Segue to a sunporch situated at the front of my grandparents' home, a large cushion lay propped up on a daybed, its backside resting on a large picture window. The year was 1934. I was seven, my sister five. We were throwing, by turns, a baseball at the cushion; our aunts and grandparents were four rooms removed, discussing the June wedding of my surrogate mother, Mary Alice. Southpaw Gloria Jo wound up, sending the horsehide through the window, at which time Gloria sprinted from the sunporch screaming at the top of her lungs, "Jackie (a sobriquet pinned on me by a great uncle who idolized heavyweight champion Jack Dempsey) threw the baseball through the window!" Quicker than my sister had negotiated the four rooms, my grandfather burst into the room and grabbing me by the scruff of the neck, proceeded to whale the living Jesus out of me. His blows interspersed by words to the effect that I was a malefactor, who, instead of having been taken in by his grandparents, should have been sent to an orphanage. My blurted attempts at explanation were met with more blows and more expressions of censure. Following the whipping, I was ordered to bed without any supper, a punishment that to a kid who was always hungry hurt more than the ass tanning.

At age five, my sister had mastered not only the art of screaming bloody murder but also the art of misrepresentation; I, much to my sorrow, usually, unwillingly was the target of my sister's perfidy. It was a scene repeated time and again; even after my grandfather died in 1937, she continued unabated her lying ways. As I aged, I became more adept at dealing with her deceits; whenever she pointed an accusatory finger my way, I would suddenly receive a message from the Holy Spirit directing me to don priestly vestments, to dedicate my life and energies to serving the Almighty, a message shared always with my very religious grandmother, who saw in me her first-class ticket on the "Heaven-Bound Express." My pronouncement spared me many an ass-chewing and the loss of victuals.

But I must be honest. It wasn't merely her lying nature or her expertise in the art of chicanery. She was a burr under my saddle blanket in other ways as well, and though it pains me to admit it, she was a far better athlete than I, an amazing tomboy, who from the age of six was a constant source of embarrassment to me. How would you feel when at the age of eight your six-year-old sister was picked for a team before you? Oh, the shame! The little bitch could hit a baseball a mile, carry a football in broken-field runs, rivaling those of the Galloping Ghost and scamper up trees like a damned monkey. The lies I could handle; the athleticism was another matter. Not content to merely outdo me, she continually taunted me with snide remarks about my lack of athletic talent as well as my gelatinous butt; however, she always managed to save her best shot for those occasions when I refused to allow her the use of my personal possessions. It was then that my lack of skills as a boxer came into play.

Following my grandfather's untimely death in 1937, my grandmother experienced great difficulty in dealing with her husband's demise, a situation compounded by her having to deal with two rambunctious kids, my sister and me; therefore, in desperation, she turned for assistance in dealing with us to people with whom she had had little or no intercourse. One such person was my stepfather's brother, Don. While my grandfather lived, Don and his wife, Toots, were never welcomed in our home, the result of Don's brother having shot to death my mother and also a nasty court battle for custody of my sister and me. They were persona non grata, but now, in light of Grandmother's situation, they were welcomed like too-long-absent friends: My grandmother, when it suited her needs, was a master of absolution. So it was that Don and Toots began numerous visits to the family domicile and thus began a ritual that began in 1937 and ended abruptly in 1941.

One of Uncle Don's pleasures during these visits was to pull two sets of boxing gloves from the trunk of his Ford coupe, after which he would lace the gloves on my sister and me and have us box a few rounds, knowing full well that Gloria would clean my plow and anything else that stood in the path of her wicked left hook. During the mismatches, held on our front lawn, Uncle, his rotund body ensconced in a lawn chair, would encourage Gloria to whip my ass, which she did with regularity. My fate would be to end up crying, blood dripping from my reddened nose, Gloria strutting around the yard, arms extended over her head, gloves together, as indication that she had once again bettered and battered her sissified pussy of a brother, while Uncle laughed his ass off. But change lay just over the horizon; this dog was going to have his day.

The summer of 1938 found my sister and I spending a few weeks of our summer vacation in Inglewood, California, as guests of Uncle Don and Aunt Toots. As usual, my sis and I were given the royal treatment by our childless uncle and aunt. Each day, we swam at the Inglewood Municipal Pool, attended at least two movies a week, ate our fill of hamburgers and hot dogs, and for two weeks were catered to, practically rendering us unfit to return to our pedestrian life with Grandmother.

Into the final week of our stay with yet no mention of "putting on the gloves," I began to breathe a little easier, thinking, hoping, that I was "out of the woods." Then, as I had feared, it happened: "Come on, Jackie, let's put on the gloves," my sister announced, contempt verily dripping from each syllable. Unable, after weak attempts to worm my way out of yet another inevitable humiliation, I, after much "oh, shuckses," and "gee-whizzes," once again found myself about to play punching bag to a sister who couldn't wait to beat the hell out of me.

Relatives and neighbors and a stray cat or two formed the ring as my uncle hit his beer bottle with his pocket knife, announcing the beginning of round one. As I warily advanced to the center of the ring (actually a lawn), I felt my yellow streak running up my spine with the rapidity of a thermometer in July; my sister, on the other hand, came out in a crouch, mayhem written all over her face; the terror in my face was the last thing she saw.

I was about two feet from her when I threw a punch, a round house, that landed with a thud right in the middle of her face, lifting her off her feet, sending her sprawling to the lawn. She didn't move. I thought she was acting, and I waited for her retaliation that I just knew was coming, then it would be I lying on the grass or worse, bawling while blood streamed from my nose's ruptured blood vessels. But why isn't she moving? Jesus! I've killed her. My uncle and aunt rushed to her side along with Old Mrs. Jones the widow from next door; in the confusion, I hauled ass, knowing full well that having murdered my sister, I would soon be taking up space in a cell on death row in the State Pen.

About two blocks from the house, I slid under a car parked on the curb, remaining there until my uncle found me, the lethal gloves still on my hands, my shirt front covered in oil dripped from the oil pan of my Detroit-assembled covert.

After my uncle had assured me that my sister was still among the living, we headed home, my uncle chuckling and shaking his head, "That was a real haymaker, Jackie." I don't know if I was thrilled to learn of my sister's escape from the jaws of death or the fact that Uncle Don, for the first time that I could remember, paid me a compliment.

The next morning, my sister showed up at the breakfast table, her left eye swollen and blackened. As she seated herself across from me, I looked up from my bowl of oatmeal, a shit-eating grin on my face. She, in turn, proffered no smart cracks about my lack of coordination or my bell-like anatomy. By her silence, she declared a truce; however, even in defeat, she was defiant. Although our brother-sister relationship never improved, becoming more strained as the two of us matured, she never again posed a threat to my masculinity.

In the words of William Shakespeare, "The smallest worm will turn, being trodden on." This worm executed a complete somersault!

FLASH

$\mathscr{I}$t was a warm spring day in 1939. Worming my way home through the back paths of town, my ears were assaulted by the unmistakable sounds of metal on wood. A row of run-down frame houses, built in another era, lay just ahead of me. Attached to each shack was a lean-to that served as a garage for those occupants of the shanties fortunate enough to own an automobile. Atop one of the lean-tos, spindle legs and sparse frame draped in too large coveralls, cloth paper-thin at knees, one shoulder strap unattached, patches on the garments seat, stood the most unkempt kid I had ever had the displeasure of seeing. In his right hand, he held a claw hammer, in his left a handful of ten penny nails, which he was feverishly pounding into the lean-tos' rickety roof.

My "What's your name, kid?" prompted a brazen, over-the-shoulder response, "Ed!" Not missing a beat, he continued pounding nails into the weathered one-by-eights that passed as a roof. "Where're you from?" From out of the din created by his hammering came a muffled "LA!" In school, I was always accounted a very good student of geography, but I had as yet not encountered any city in the United States called LA. I deduced that he either suffered a speech impediment, or he was from the state of Louisiana; both notions, I was to discover, were incorrect: He could speak clearly, and he was not from the South but rather from Los Angeles, a claim he never let us country bumpkins forget. But as I was quickly to learn he was also a spinner of wild tales, a fact that my initial contact with him bore out.

Once the ice was broken and I had established that he was not orally handicapped and that he hailed from pre-smog "City of the Angels," I began the typical interrogation to which all new kids were subjected: his age, his favorite sports, the amount of his weekly allowance, his grade, and his father's occupation. He was fourteen; his sports, basketball and baseball, his allowance zilch, an eighth grader. It was with my last feeler that I had trouble. "My dad?

He's in Africa hunting lions and wildebeest." My jaw must have noticeably dropped about five inches. By the looks of this kid's clothes, I thought his old man must have been having a rough year. Turning on my heels, I headed for home and supper, my empty stomach overruling the urge to stay and be treated to more hokum.

The next time I encountered Ed was during lunch period at our junior high. In between bites of a sandwich, he was regaling his audience of seventh graders with accounts of his athletic prowess. "Yeh, I hit four home runs in one game when I lived in LA," he boasted, portions of his egg salad sandwich lodged between the gaps of his crooked teeth. "Once," he continued, "I punted a football eighty yards. Howard Jones SC's head coach said I could play for the Trojans any time." The underclassmen were wide-eyed. Finished with his lunch, Ed wadded up his lunch sack, hook-shot it into a trash can some twenty feet away, and began to walk toward the outdoor basketball courts, his troupe of lemmings close at heel hanging on his every saw. I stood rooted to the ground, amazed at my classmate's ignorance. Here was a guy barely five foot five, weighing perhaps 115 pounds laying claim to athletic feats that put baseball's Lou Gehrig and football's Sammy Baugh to shame. But Ed, despite his very active imagination, would one day prove a hero of a different ilk.

While I'm about it, I had best explain how Ed got the nickname "Flash." Playing basketball one winter's day in the company of my uncle Sedgwick, Ed unconsciously hooked a shot from half-court, the ball getting nothing but net. Uncle Sedgwick ever the guy to tack nicknames on people (mine was "lard ass"), quickly dubbed Ed with the sobriquet "Flash," and "Flash" it remains to this day.

But I alluded to Ed as a hero of another ilk. His dad may not have been a great white hunter, but Ed was more heroic than the persona he conjured from his imagination. A late-in-life child, Ed was disliked by his mother, whose constant badgering was not only dispiriting to him but also a source of embarrassment to his chums who would occasionally play around his house. She was a termagant woman.

At age fifteen, tired of his mother's browbeating, Ed decided it was time to leave home, a practice of many young people during the Depression years. Anyway, Ed got his mother to sign an affidavit declaring that Ed was sixteen and half, which in turn got him into the navy. He didn't have to beg his mother; she was happy to be rid of him.

The first reports we got were that Ed was missing in the Pearl Harbor raid; later we were to learn that he had been taken prisoner by the Japanese at Wake Island. Ed spent the duration of World War II working in Japanese factories and mines on the Japanese mainland where he was beaten and starved by his captors. Released at war's end, he remained in the navy, married a young lady from the eastern seaboard, and began a family. Quite suddenly, he contracted polio putting him out of the navy and into a wheelchair where he remains today.

Through it all, the prisoner of war years, the debilitating disease, the loss of his sight, the result of the many beatings he suffered at the hands of his Japanese captors, Ed has remained upbeat, working various jobs, raising a family, and in general leading a fulfilling life. Old Flash has lived up to the nickname pinned on him some sixty years ago, the day he made that bucket from half-court.

MEA CULPA

$\mathscr{T}$hough never mentioned in either the Old or New Testaments, it was gospel in Hispanic families that when a male child received a calling to the cloth, his parents were guaranteed a suite in heaven. So it was with my Spanish grandmother, she who had been convent educated in the province of Galicia where under the tutelage of the good nuns learned to needlepoint, pray the rosary, supplicate the saints for guidance, and remain chaste until such time that she would wed a man schooled, with the exception of the needlepoint, in much the same manner. So what did Grandmother do? She married an American Presbyterian, who from early childhood had been religiously nurtured on the teachings of John Calvin. But I digress.

In the small border community of my youth, more than half the population was Roman Catholic. Many of my non-Catholic chums, fearing ostracism, claimed they were "right-handers," going so far as to occasionally attend Mass, study the Baltimore Catechism under the heavy hand of Sister Mary Joseph, and wear green on Saint Patrick's Day.

But there was one thing they couldn't do—become altar boys. They could join the Bobby Benson B Bar B riders club; they could be initiated into Orphan Annie's Secret Society, and they could even acquire membership in Jimmy Allen's Aviation Club, but they, because of lack of a baptismal certificate, and first Holy Communion and confirmation, could not gain admittance to the exclusive fraternity of the surplice and cassock. They would never proudly sport the pin that identified you as a server, never share in the rewards of trips to the beach, hamburgers and fries, the one-and two-dollar tips meted out to those of us fortunate enough to have assisted the priests at baptisms and weddings. It was a fruit those poor, heretical wretches would never savor; however, the role of the acolyte was not all skittles and beer!

Before you were allowed into the sacristy, before you were entrusted the job of firing up, the incense in the censer, but more importantly, you had to commit to memory all the responses of the Mass—*in Latin!* And this is where, as I perceived it at the time, my dear grandmother had the door to her reserved room in God's heavenly lodge slammed in her presumptuous Castilian face.

Following the untimely deaths of our parents, my sister and I were brought into our grandparents' home where we were placed into the care of our two aunts, Mary Alice and Eveline. A few years later, legally adopted, we assumed the Bowman surname. Prior to our orphanhood, neither my sister nor I had been introduced to any form of religious training, and although we both had been baptized in the Roman Catholic faith, neither of us had seen the inside of a church since. Enter granddad and his Bible-belt theology.

His newly acquired progeny was going to attend church, any church, just so long as it was not controlled by Rome. Because the nearest Presbyterian church was some fifteen miles removed from our community, we were enrolled in Sunday school classes at the local Community church at which time my devout RC grandmother quickly hied herself, rosary in hand, to Our Lady of Mount Carmel parish where she put match to every unlit votive candle, repeatedly struck her breast while reciting in Spanish every prayer she knew, repeating her orisons in broken English, pleading with the Blessed Mother and all the saints to sabotage granddad's efforts to wean my sister and me from the heretical influences of the papacy. We attended the congregational Sunday school sessions for the ensuing five years. So much for grandmother's pull in heaven.

Following my grandfather's death in 1937, grandmother decided that if the Blessed Mother and the saints were going to sit on their hands and make no effort to salvage the religious lives of her two innocents, she would. We were summarily introduced to Mother Superior who wasted little time enrolling us in afternoon catechism classes. (Question: Who made the world . . . Answer: God made the world) which upon completion would allow us to receive our first Holy Communion, after which we would be receiving confirmation. Granddad must have been turning in his grave! Once confirmed, I was eligible to join the altar boy society where it was expected that you have clean hands, never be late, and commit the Latin responses to memory. The clean hands and punctuality I could deal with, but it was the Latin that eventually pricked my adolescent conscience. I committed to memory all the Latin responses save one: the "Confiteor." I mumbled my way through that prayer for more than three years, and as I struck my breast three times, reciting as I did "Mea culpa, mea culpa, mea maxima culpa," I just knew that the Masses at which I assisted were null and void and that the parishioners at those masses would be turned away on Judgment Day! But more disturbing was the thought that my poor, trusting grandmother had placed her dream of a heavenly hereafter into the hands of a total religious ingrate! *Mea culpa!*

My sister, Gloria Jo, and me (1930)

Grandfather, Grandmother, my infant mother, Josephine (Mexico, 1907)

Mother and Mary Alice (Mexico, 1911)

Mother (1930)

The Bungalow (Chula Vista, CA)

Aunt Mary Alice, high school graduation (1932)

Grandfather: A man of great integrity (1933)

Grand Uncle, Grand Aunt and Grandfather (1933)

Caliente race track before the Socialists took office,
"Destination of Hollywood's Beautiful People." (circa 1930)
(File on disk from San Diego Historical Society)

The Foreign Club, Tijuana, Mexico (circa 1930)

Tent City (Coronado, CA, circa 1932) "Grandpa didn't trust any young man wearing a fraternity pin." *(File on disk from San Diego Historical Society)*

Uncle Sam (me) and Miss Liberty (Gloria Jo),
Miss Cramp's kindergarten
(Fourth of July, 1932)

Family gathering at San Pedro aboard French cargo ship: left to right, Grandfather, Grandmother, Mary Alice, Great Grandfather, Great Grandmother, Grandmother, Aunt Eveline (Babe), Jack (me) and Gloria Jo (1931)

Yoo Have a Charming Place Here

I have known priests, and I have known priests; however, the one cleric who stands hands above the many with whom I have been acquainted was the pastor at Our Lady of Mount Carmel, Father Joseph P. O'Leary. In recent years, it has become de rigueur to criticize anyone wearing a collar because of the perverted actions of a few members of the cloth; Father Ryan wore his priestly serge with great dignity and a devoted compassion for his flock. He did, however, have one failing: He was as naive as a newborn, a trait that leads me into this episode.

Father Ryan came to our parish fresh off the boat from Ireland, with a short layover in New York where he attended Fordham University, studying Spanish, preparing him for his assignment in Southern California, where one out of four Roman Catholics was of Mexican descent. Our parish, but a few thousand yards from the international border, was, with few exceptions, composed of Hispanics, my half sister and I being two of the "few exceptions," and we both were one-third Spanish on our mother's side. Although the masses were said in Latin, the homilies were delivered in Spanish, which was all well and good when our priests' surnames were a roll call of the forces of Pancho Villa, but we had never, until 1938, had an Anglo as our shepherd.

It was in 1938 that Father Ryan stepped up to the pulpit giving his homily in pure lisping Castilian Spanish. The parishioners were dumbfounded, being that most of them spoke border patois! But language proved but a minor problem, and within a year, Father Tim was speaking border-speak like a Tijuana street taco vendor. My first real contact with the good father was during my stint as an altar boy and a member of the Altar Boys' Society, an organization upon which father placed much responsibility for its assistance at weddings, baptisms, funerals, and especially for serving at Mass, novenas, and stations of the cross. Our services were rewarded in many ways, but perhaps the best reward of all was the annual Altar Boy picnic usually held twice a year, in the early fall and late spring. Father would load us all into his DeSoto touring sedan and head for the mountains or the seashore where we would enjoy a day of hiking, swimming, ball playing, and eating to the bursting point, the picnic lunch provided by the parish mothers. It was really the eating we all looked forward to, the lunch consisting of a plethora of culinary delights: tacos, tamales, tortillas, refritos, with a bag of Mexican *pan dulce* (sweet bread) for dessert.

Late spring in 1939 ushered in a period of extreme heat for that time of the year, a cyclical occurrence in Southern California brought on by Santa Ana winds blowing off the desert. And because of the temperatures, it was decided that our annual excursion would be to the beach, to the Silver Strand, at that time a sliver of sand and seaside vegetation over whose surface a two-lane road ran connecting the communities of the South Bay with the village of Coronado, separating the Pacific Ocean from San Diego Bay.

All was preparedness. The DeSoto, packed with balls and bats, beach balls, a beach umbrella, towels, beach blankets and six squirming altar boys, Father Joseph at the wheel headed west toward our destination some fifteen miles distance. Father in his black serge suit, black fedora, and priestly collar was hardly dressed for a day at the beach, but he seemed not concerned as he joined his band of young brigands in a rousing chorus of "By the Beautiful Sea," his rich tenor voice punctuated by his strong Irish brogue.

Playtime and swimming over, we boys sat ourselves in a circle around the beach blanket while Father headed for the car and the victuals, the thought of which had us drooling down the fronts of our T-shirts. Suddenly we heard Father cry out, "Holy Mother of Jesus, we forgot to pack the lunch!" Forgot the lunch? Father, arms flailing the air, was performing an Irish jig up and down from the car's rear bumper to its grill, all the while shouting strange oaths, "There's a crimple in the sprood o' me doogan's," or something that sounded like that. We all knew it wasn't High Mass Latin, but we also knew that it sounded the knell for our much anticipated repast. Finally, after five or so minutes of jigging and "oathing," Father trudged back to our deflated assemblage, ruefully announcing that we would have to make other plans if we were to eat lunch.

Beach paraphernalia and kids loaded into the DeSoto, Father headed posthaste for downtown Coronado. It is well to note that in the 1930s, the Crown City still had one foot in the Victorian Era; therefore, Sundays offered very little in the way of entertainment, or, for that matter, places to eat. Restaurants and theaters were closed on the Sabbath, a practice instituted by the Methodist founders of the resort, a practice that went by the boards with the advent of World War II. It was also the era of BFF (before fast food). So where did that leave the good Father? With six ravenous youngsters threatening to eat the car's upholstery, Father frantically searched for a beanery, any beanery, to feed his charges who even as they cruised up and down Orange Avenue seemed on the verge of turning cannibalistic. Then as if in answer to his orisons, he spotted it—The Blue Moon Bar and Grill, a dingy storefront sporting two smudged porthole-like windows set into the peeling wood siding on either side of the recessed entrance.

The DeSoto parked, passengers disgorged, Father quickly herded us into the enveloping darkness of the saloon, our nostrils assaulted by a mixture of alcohol, cigarette smoke, and human effluvium, our ears by the tinkling of glass, choice profanities, wanton whoops, and raucous screeches, punctuated by the ping-pinging of a pinball machine.

When at last adjusted to the murkiness, our eyes riveted on cleavage, a veritable chasm between the largest breasts anyone of us had ever seen, heaving milk-white dubbies not found in the Sears catalog. "Can I help you, Father?" the barmaid asked, revealing the absence of one of her central incisors. Father replied that we were in need of some sustenance and if she would kindly place our order for hamburgers, chips (he meant fries), and soft drinks. "But, Father, we're a bar, not a restaurant." Undaunted, Father asked her if the bar served food. "Yes, we do, but the boys are under age and legally they can't be served here." Father assured the barmaid that he would be responsible for us and she should not fret. Shrugging her shoulders, she placed our order with the cook standing at his grill, spatula at the ready. The four booze guzzlers seated on the barstools looked on in rapt silence and amazement as Father seated the six of us in a booth, grabbed a chair from one of the small tables positioned in the center of the saloon, and, having deposited his fedora on one of the numerous hooks attached to the wall, seated himself at the head of the booth's rectangular table.

The odor of beef and onions wafting into our booth like an invisible mist assaulted our olfactory sense, whetting our appetites to a sharpness—the lunch, huge triple-decked hamburgers. (We deduced from the hamburgers' size that the cook was either a "right-hander" or nearsighted)—with all the trimmings were, after what seemed like the running time of a High Mass, delivered, prayed over, and without ceremony bolted down in record time under the incredulous gaze of the customers bellied up to the oaken bar, after which Father rousted us and our grease-begrimed faces out of the booth, paid the check, and pointed us toward the door. "Yoo hav' a charmin' place here," he imparted to our buxom serving maid, turned, and followed us out into the blinding sunlight of downtown Coronado.

I have it on good authority that Father Joseph, as a chaplain with the Fourth Infantry Division in World War II, participated in the invasion of Fortress Europe in the third wave at Normandy, serving the spiritual needs of his troops through the VE Day. I have often envisioned him in Paris at one of the notorious bistros in Place Pigalle remarking to one of the scantily clad showgirl, "Yoo hav' a charmin' place here."

ONLY THE OLD DIE

When I was four and a half, my parents had met a tragic end, but as I was still an innocent; their passing had been to some extent an abstraction. Although my grandfather's death proved traumatic, I had never experienced the death of someone of my own age. Only the old died, and my friends and I were young. It was the death of Oscar Noriega, one of my childhood pals, that brought home the sobering realization that I was mortal, his death scaring the hell out of me. Death had at long-last shed the vestiges of the abstract. Oscar was ten; so was I. "When we are young, we think not only of ourselves, but that all about us are immortal," Benjamin Disraeli said.

What I remember most about Oscar, aside from his nickname "Boxcars," a sobriquet more in keeping with his large ass rather than its rhyme, was his skill in shooting baskets. There wasn't a kid attending San Ysidro Elementary School who could beat him in a game of "horses." He hit baskets from every point in the perimeter. Basketball skills aside, Oscar was one of the nicest kids in school; everyone liked him, students and teachers alike.

Saturday morning in early spring of 1936, an extremely warm day in April, the gang decided to head for the large pond at the end of Dairy Mart Road. The pond, fed by the waters of the pre-cesspool days of the Tijuana River, was encircled by willows, an ideal spot for skinny-dipping; it also held a fairly good population of small bass and bluegill.

After an afternoon of swimming, angling, and comparing anatomical attributes, such as they were, we headed home by way of Sunset Boulevard., planning to pilfer some half-ripe peaches from old man Simmons's fruit trees, and having gorged ourselves on the half-ripened fruit, we happily headed home, stopping along the way to deposit in a roadside mailbox two shriveled and malodorous bluegill we'd managed to catch at the pond. The four of us agreed to meet for some basketball the next afternoon.

Sunday afternoon found three of our group shooting baskets on the playground basketball court. But where was Oscar? It wasn't like him to miss our regular Sunday game, especially since he could clean all of us.

After an hour of halfhearted half-court, we decided to drop by Oscar's house. His mom informed us that her son was laid up with a very severe stomach ache—the green peaches! Oscar, as was his wont, ate more than us, so it just figured he would be sick, but all of us at one time or another had suffered upset stomachs from too much unripened fruit, so we paid his malady little thought and went on our way.

On Monday morning, Oscar's fifth grade desk was unoccupied, nor was he in it on Tuesday. Wednesday morning, Mrs. Morse, our teacher, announced to the class that Oscar had died. He had died at home, his Depression-poor family unable to pay for a doctor, (knowing Dr. Brown's reputation, Oscar might have died anyway). Later we learned from a neighbor's daughter that Mrs. Noriega, thinking that Oscar had no more than a bad upset stomach, had placed hot compresses on his stomach, resulting in a ruptured appendix. "Holy Mother of Christ," I anguished, "would I be next?" The entire school was stunned. This was an era when kids were forced to deal with their traumas without the assistance of priests, rabbis, or counselors. Each of us had to deal with Oscar's passing on our own or in my case with the members of my group. I don't recall any one kid crying with the exception of Calvin Henry, who cried on the slightest pretext.

Certainly we were all saddened to have lost Oscar, and his death was a source of preoccupation for quite a while. Me? It proved really the first time that I began worrying about my own life and its natural end, more so than the deaths of my parents.

One wag in our group summed up what many of us were really thinking about Oscar's passing, "Shit! Boxcar could sure shoot baskets."

THE MOTHER OF ALL KITES

Young men think old men are fools,
but old men know young men are fools.

—George Chapman

*T*raditionally the month of March ushered in one of childhood's favorite pastimes: kite flying. On any given afternoon, kites of every imaginable color, shape, and size dotted the clear, blue spring sky of my neighborhood. There was the homemade kite, easily identified by its newspaper covering, the store-bought kite with its airplane logo, the artistic kid's creation, red and green Christmas wrapping paper, serrated notches fluttering along the kite's diamond-shaped structure. Then there were the tails, long, short, some made from old rags, others collections of men's neckwear.

The boys, and an occasional girl, controlled the kite's movements by line attached to its midsection, the line ranging from the fifty-yard spool of regular kite string to knotted pieces of string and cord of varying diameters. The more sophisticated kite jockeys, usually the older fellas, flew their kites with fishing rods and line filched from their father's tackle closet, allowing them to simply reel in their flyers much in the manner one reels in a fish.

My friend, Bob, ever the inventive guy, quickly tired of the same old routines employed by most of the Seaward Avenue gang: kite fights, the kites fitted with razor blades for shredding other combatants' kites, ground glass liberally sprinkled on lines coated with glue or paste, Kleenex parachutes weighted with nuts or washers to which a bent pin or fishhook was attached and placed upside down, allowing the wind to propel the chute up the line to a point just before reaching the kite the line was jerked and the parachute freed to float freely to the ground. Bob, tired of these mundane activities, began searching his beehive-like brain for more exciting, more novel avenues of expression. Thus was born the idea for an eight-foot box kite!

Bob's plan was simple. We, he and I, would construct a box kite that would prove a flying invention rivaling the flying contraptions envisioned by Leonardo da Vinci. The plan was to build a kite big and strong enough to lift a small-bodied human into the firmament, and I was elected the body designate!

Gathering lath, tissue paper, string, and glue, we began constructing what we envisioned would prove a kite rivaling Ben Franklin's. Weeks of cutting, sanding, and gluing in my grandfather's garage produced a kite, the envy of every boy in town—eight feet tall, covered with green and red paper glued over a structure of lath and molding pilfered from various building sites, all held together by a network of braided fishing line removed from my uncle's saltwater fishing reel. We felt proud at what we had achieved; my grandfather, ever the pragmatist, felt we had taken leave of our senses: "You'll need a wind of hurricane force to get that damned thing off the ground!" Grandfather proved a seer. The kite stood in the garage for more than two years, its paper covering reduced to shreds limply hanging from its frame, mute testimony to our crackpot scheme.

But Bob and I could always lay claim to have constructed the "Mother of all Kites!"

ANYONE HERE NEED A
135-POUND JOCKEY?

---

*I*n an earlier sketch, I recounted having spent portions of my summer vacations in the care of my stepuncle Don Long and his wife, Toots. Their twenty-year union childless, the couple, for the years 1938-41, took my sister and me in tow for four glorious weeks during summer vacation where the two of us had our every desire granted: new clothes for the fall school term, a much needed new bicycle tire, movies twice weekly, our stomachs full of hamburgers, French fries, and gallons of ice cream; in other works, the two of us teetered on the brink of adolescent hedonism.

For those four summers, during the horse racing seasons at Hollywood Park and Del Mar, we escaped the dysfunctional and verbal abuse environs of our home to contently wallow in an environment awash with love, generosity, and understanding. At vacation's end, it was difficult to return "home." It was during this period in my life that I became obsessed with the idea of becoming a jockey. There was, however, one slight problem: At age twelve, I weighed 135 pounds!

Not overly fond of Don because of what his brother had down to her eldest daughter, my Spanish grandmother was not above farming us scalawags out for a few weeks each summer, perhaps secretly hoping that Don and Toots would kidnap the two of us, relieving her of the responsibility of raising us, something for which she was ill fit. Grandma had neither the patience nor the know-how to deal with us. So off we went those four summers first to Inglewood for two weeks and following those two week to Del Mar.

Although the nation and its citizenry were in the early years of the Depression, sister dear and I knew full well that Uncle Don was in the chips, at least in our child's minds we reckoned he was. Didn't he buy a new Ford coupe

---

every two years? We, therefore, deduced that he could pick up the tab for some of our frivolous requests. A jockey's valet, he and Aunt Toots traveled the length of California, he working the racing seasons at Tanforan and Bay Meadows in the Bay Area and Southern California's three tracks, Santa Anita, Hollywood Park, and Del Mar, where he made a good living tending to the needs of the jockeys placed in his care. His duties included keeping tack (saddles), boots, and racing clothing in good order. Aunt Toots? She came along for the ride.

Until my sister and I began spending those glorious weeks with them, it was their custom to rent an apartment for their stay during the racing meets; however, with two added bodies to shelter, they began renting homes, many with extra rooms, which they would rent to low-paid apprentice jockeys. So, you ask, what does all that talk about real estate have to do with my wanting to be a jockey? Patience my dear reader, I shall explain.

In the summer of 1938, Hollywood Park opened for its inaugural racing season, and a few weeks into the meet, Uncle Don and Aunt Toots were in our living rooms requesting that G randmother allow them to take Gloria Jo and me to Inglewood for two weeks; they didn't have to beg for permission. Two hours later our little bags were packed. We were motoring north on Highway 101, my head swimming with thought of a summer of swimming, movies, great food, and most importantly, large portions of love, unfretted freedom, and something I hadn't planned on.

Lodging with my aunt and uncle was an apprentice jockey named Wallace Leischman, a young man of seventeen, a jockey in the making whose demeanor was unlike most of the wearers of racing silks. Many of the jockeys I had encountered on my visits to the jockeys' room at the track were ill-educated reprobates shooting pool, cigarettes hanging from their snarling lips, their mouths spilling profanities in layers, and being sarcastic and egocentric.

Wallace, the antithesis of that crowd, was a serious young man, his brush with the profane and occasional "gosh." It was he who encouraged my first thoughts of becoming a jockey, and despite my corpulent figure, he didn't scoff at my announcement that I ended to be a rider; no, in the tone of a big brother, he went along with my plans, advising my to watch what I ate; however, his support of my plans also included a gift I shall never forget.

About midway through my first week with Uncle and Aunt, Wallace called me into his room, handed me a pair of oversize cowboy boots, and one of his old sweaters, the two-toned style worn by backstretch personnel and especially by exercise boys and grooms, the light wool sweater sporting leather-elbow patches; more importantly, the outer garment smelled of racetrack, backstretch "cologne," the blended odor of warm horse manure, hay, saddle-soup leather, and the warm, rich fragrance of a horse newly washed and groomed. To complete this raiment, Aunt Toots bought me a Western-styled shirt (plaid-pattered, imitation pearl snap buttons on cuffs and shirt front) the kind worn by jockey George Woolf. Not only did I look the part but I also smelled the part.

For the next week, attired in my "new" duds, I accompanied my uncle to the track's jockeys' room, the oversize boots creating a plopping cadence as I wandered the facility, hoping that a jockey or jockeys would take notice of me, but aside from a few snide remarks and snickers, I went unnoticed, that is until one of the smart-asses burst my bubble, "Hey, Jack, who'd you steal them boots from?" But thanks to Wallace, I was provided the experience that made a successful summer of 1938.

Three days before my sister and I were scheduled to return home, Wallace asked me if I would like a couple of hots the next day. Walk hots? You bet! (By way of explanation, a "hot" is a horse who, worked out in the morning, must be walked until cooled.) "I've talked to my trainer, and he says you can walk at least one hot tomorrow morning and maybe two. You'll get two bits a hot." Wallace stood back, awaiting my answer. "You bet," I said. So smitten was I with the idea I would have walked hots for nothing.

Early the next morning about 4:00 a.m., Wallace rousted me out of bed, instructing me to dress and meet him out on the street where his trainer was picking us up. After a stop for sinker and coffee at a local all-night diner, we were off to the back stretch, and though I had on occasion assisted my uncle in the jockeys' room cleaning and polishing tack and boots, this morning would be my first real racetrack job.

I walked three horses that morning, one mare and two geldings, earning the princely sum of six bits (seventy-five cents). It proved the first and last time that I cooled a thoroughbred, but the memory of that day so many years past lives on, securely planted in my aging brain, the memory of a fat kid who wanted to be a jockey and the young race rider's concern for that kid.

Tragically, Wallace Leischman was killed in a two-horse spill at Bay Meadows in 1939. He was only nineteen years of age.

PS: By the time I was old enough (sixteen) to be a jockey, I weighed 150 pounds.

III
The Forties

A HOUSE IS NOT A HOME

*I*s this the home of Jack Bowman? Jeez, I thought, I haven't been called Jack since I was a kid. Who in the hell could it be? Laying suspicion aside, my curiosity whetted, I barked, "Who wants to know?"

"Jack, it's Carlito Velazquez."

Carlito Velazquez! Hell, hadn't heard that name in almost seventy years (sixty-eight years to be exact), the last time in the spring of 1941 as I stood on the porch of the Velazquez family's clapboard home in San Ysidro, California. Having established who he was, Carlos and I talked, and as we jawed about the days of our youth spent in a small border town located but a few miles from Tijuana, Mexico, my mind wandered to another time, an unhappy time, when I lived in a dysfunctional family, when I lived in a house that was not a home, resulting in my seeking love and acceptance in other households, with other families.

Enter the Velazquez family who embraced me as one of their own, welcomed me into their fold, provided the love I didn't receive at home. Mrs. Velazquez was especially kind, greeting me as I entered her kitchen with a warm and loving, "Buenos Dias, Yaky" and an equally warm, right-off-the stove flour tortilla. A few pleasant greetings exchanged, and Joe, the family's third eldest son, and I were off to school. My nickname as a child was Jack, most folks preferring to call me Jackie, which would explain Mrs. Velazquez's Spanish pronunciation of the name. A tiny lady, she possessed a kind heart, with room for me, and I am certain she loved me as she loved her own children.

The Velazquez family was large: father, mother, four daughters, and five sons, all living in an old frame house that, including the small kitchen, consisted of four small rooms, the yard, a pile of dirt, rocks, and weeds, an outhouse set in the backyard like a huge malodorous exclamation point; conversely, my family's house was a pretty, white California stucco (architecture popular in the late

1920s and 1930s), three bedrooms, a large living room, dining room, a large, well-appointed kitchen, two bathrooms, and a sunporch. The yard, a manicured lawn, flower beds in profusion, and trees of every shape, every height, all neatly ensconced within a white picket fence in addition to a three-car garage. So, you might ask, why did I prefer spending my days in a run-down shanty when our house was cleaner, more attractive, and much roomier? The shanty and its occupants gave a lonely, unwanted child the love and acceptance he craved, things denied to him by the members of his own family; conversely, his house was not a home but a place filled with unhappiness, cross words, perpetual criticism, and, perhaps most noticeable, the absence of the phrase, "I love you, Jack." But the unkindness cut of all occurred on my fourteenth birthday, the day the family decided I should join the navy, so anxious to be rid of me, they were willing to swear I was sixteen and a half.

The more they talked, the more convinced was I that a career as a swab jock would be an improvement over the life I was living. One afternoon in the spring of 1941, I was unceremoniously presented to a navy recruiter, a chief petty officer, with duty stripes extending from his uniform jacket's cuff to the bend in his elbow, an unlit cigar stub that gripped between yellowed molars, a stogie that looked and smelled like a three-day-old dog turd, his appearance so wizened he might well have been Admiral Dewey's yeoman. "Are you ladies certain that you want to this young man in Uncle Sam's Navy?" They were.

Brazenly shoving the bogus certificate under the CPO's bulbous nose, they retreated two steps from the desk where they both stood like two crows looking over a roadkill. Me? Forgotten, left staring blankly out a window onto Broadway, three stories below, my eyes riveted on a Number Eleven streetcar disgorging passengers at Horton Plaza, my mind insensitive, the verbal exchange between Grandma, Aunt, and chief petty officer only a garbled noise. Finally, the chief's stentorian voice put a lid on the proceedings, "Ladies, stop this nonsense! I don't care what that affidavit says. That kid is no older than twelve or thirteen years of age, and if you think I am going send him to boot camp, you're crazy!"

Thanks to the CPO, I got a reprieve, and although I wasn't going into the navy, I was going back into that loveless environment provided by my family. I did, however, have an "ace in the hole." There was still Mrs. V and her loving brood to provide me the love my family couldn't or simply wouldn't give me. I believe to this day had it not been for the love and understanding I received from this hardscrabble Mexican family, my life would have been more of a mess than it was. A few years after the USN experience, I departed San Ysidro, and the loving family Velazquez; never did I think I would I return, never to be embraced in the loving arms of that diminutive Mexican lady; at least that's what I thought in 1941. Fate, however, had other ideas.

It was spring of 1960—graduation day for me and twenty of my classmates from the University of San Diego, College for Men. Having gone through the ceremony and received my degree, I ambled up the stairway, with my wife, leading to the campus concourse, eager to disrobe and head into Mission Valley for a celebratory drink (or two) and a quiet candlelight dinner. Reaching the top rung, I noticed movement out of the corner of my eye; turning, I noticed a Mexican family standing on the sidewalk, eyes focused on me, and directly in the middle of the gathering stood a small, gray-haired lady, eyes riveted on me. My god, I thought, it can't be! It was! There she was, my diminutive surrogate mother, walking in tiny steps toward me, a smile upon her face, a twinkle in her eyes. "Yaky, como esta usted, hijo?" Hugging her, I replied that I was well (in Spanish, of course). Throwing her arms around my waist, she pressed her head against my chest and said, "Ah, mi hijo, mi hijo." I was her son and would ever be. Though she has been gone these many years, when I pray the Prayer of the Faithful at Sunday Mass, I make it a point to thank God for having blessed me with a loving, sheltering mother hen who provided me a home, made me a member of her large brood, and loved me as one of her chicks.

JITTERBUG

The greater the fool, the better the dancer.

—Theodore Hook

At Southwest Junior High, each school month was highlighted by a school dance held in the school's auditorium. SJHS was to my knowledge the only educational institution, junior or senior high, that had its own jukebox to provide dance music for our monthly sock hops; unfortunately, the person in charge of the machine, the person upon whose shoulders lay the responsibility of record selection was Mrs. Bruce, our esteemed music teacher, who deemed jitterbugging the first step to eternal damnation. Therefore, we students were subjected to a never-ending parade of music by the likes of Wayne King, Horace Height and his Musical Knights, the Swing and Sway rhythms of Sammy Kaye when all the rug-cutters wanted were heavy doses of Glenn Miller, Tommy Dorsey, and Benny Goodman. Of course, there were exceptions.

David Walton who possibly learned to waltz while womb-bound loved Mickey Mouse music; it provided him yet another opportunity to show us heavy-footed underlings how light of foot he was. But we were forced to give the devil his due—the bastard could dance, and aided by Mrs. Bruce's music selections, he had plenty of opportunity. On the dance floor, he had all the moves of a Fred Astaire sans Ginger. But lest this piece turn into a paean of Walton's skills a fourteen-year-old terpsichorean whiz, I had best get back to my subject—me.

The antithesis of "lightfoot" Walton, I was noted for my clumsiness. Built like a small version of the Liberty Bell, I was narrow on top and flared at the bottom. The sobriquet pinned on me by my uncle was lard ass. It wasn't until I had reached the age of sixteen that I acquired my Adonis-like physique, my gelatinous butt transformed into a hard-muscled gluteus. But as a youngster, my lack of physical grace as well as a severe case of advanced acne made me, in the eyes of distaff members of my class, an untouchable, doomed to spend the dances holding up a wall in the auditorium, in a word, a male wallflower. So month after month, dance after dance, I sorrowfully watched as my buddies two-four timing it around the floor, their tentacle-like arms wrapped around the delightfully blossoming bodies of our class nymphs. For months, this had been my routine, but change was in the offing.

It was our first dance following Easter vacation. I had taken up my regular station against the wall, attempting to conceal my disappointment at not being asked to dance. Suddenly someone grabbed my hand. "Come on, Jack, I'm going to teach you to dance!" Towering over me stood the five foot six inch tall Michiko Furuta, one of our numerous classmates of Japanese American descent and the eighth grade's resident brain. She was also the nicest person girl in our class. She was not only tall but also very beautiful, and had it not been for the rampant racism that existed at the time, there was not a boy in our class who wouldn't have made a play for her. And here she was, literally dragging me onto the dance floor, and despite my having been reared by a grandfather who was a bonafide racist, I had, at a very young age, come to judge people on their individual qualities not on the color of their skin, their religious beliefs or, in the case of Miss Furuta, the shape of their eyes.

Feigning unwillingness, I self-consciously and sheepishly allowed myself to be dragged to the center of the floor where she announced that I was to lead. Lead!? Quickly realizing that I had not the foggiest notion of what she meant, Michiko patiently explained that my role was to set our course, hers to follow. Easier said than done Mme. Butterfly. But she persisted, and it wasn't too long before she and I were dancing a passable waltz.—back, side, together, forward, side, together. Then, quite suddenly and without warning, Wayne King's "The Waltz You Saved for Me" was replaced by the unmistakable reed leads, saxes and clarinets, of Glenn Miller's Orchestra playing "In the Mood." It seemed that while Mrs. Bruce was visiting the ladies' powder room, some scamp had sneaked onto the stage where the jukebox was positioned and had punched the selection key for the Miller tune, and we were to learn to our joy and Mrs. Bruce's dismay a Goodman tune, a Dorsey tune, a Chick Webb tune et al. Before I realized what was happening, Miss M and I were jitterbugging. By the time Mrs. Bruce returned, pandemonium reigned! Arms and legs flailing in all directions, blurred saddle shoes twisting and pivoting at odds with the floor, seemingly attempting to escape earth's gravitation, students were doing the Lindy and the Balboa Shuffle, that is everyone but Walton, who stood forlornly on the sideline gritting his molars, convinced that the school's cretins had somehow managed to sabotage his well-laid plans to upstage us with his waltzing talents. He stayed off the floor for some time, snorting through his aristocratic nostrils and making snide remarks to his coterie of sycophants.

Me? I had found my niche. I was a born jitterbugger, a kid born to rug-cut, and owed it all to Michiko, who, I am saddened to say, ended up at Manzinar in early 1942. I never saw her again, but even today, I think of her often and with deep affection for the role she played in my rite of passage.

SOUTHERN BELL(E) AS IN DING-DONG

Ignorance, Madam, pure ignorance.

—Samuel Johnson

*D*uring my first six years of formal education, I was fortunate to have received instruction from two outstanding ladies, Miss Cramp, my kindergarten teacher, and Mrs. Corbett, my sixth grade instructor. Both ladies, each lady totally dedicated to her chosen profession, played important roles in my intellectual development. Miss Cramp had me reading before I was five; Mrs. Corbett, as you have been apprised in a previous episode, instilled in me not only an appreciation of the liberal arts, but also, and perhaps more importantly, a confidence in my worth, a quality I had sorely lacked until I came under her firm but fair guidance.

Then along came Miss Gilstrap, the poorest example of a teacher I have ever encountered. It was she who initially soured me on education, a state of mind eventually leading to my dropping out of high school midway through the second semester of my junior year. So disenchanted was I with education, I enlisted in the military, certain that death on a foreign battlefield would be preferable to sitting, day after day, in classrooms devoid of thought, with teachers of Miss Gilstrap's ilk whose ideas of educating America's youth extended no further than reading insipid articles in Junior Scholastic magazine, writing yawn-inducing book reports, and taking moronic true, false, and multiple choice tests and being assigned readings far beyond our ken, a carbon copy of my year spent on Miss Gilstrap's roll book.

Miss Gilstrap—from my first day in her class, I was quick to realize ours would not be a happy or a fruitful relationship. First of all, she spoke with an annoying Southern drawl, "y'all" being her favorite expression when addressing us. She dulled our senses with countless inane stories of her childhood, her narratives sprinkled liberally with the word "niggah" when referring to her parents' servants, and she recounted her many trips to "Nu Awluns" for Mardi Gras. Her never-ending procession of stories of her "Granfawtha's" heroics against the hated Yankees had many of my classmates believing that the CSA had defeated Mr. Lincoln's Union troops. She idolized Lee, hated Grant. As bad as her autobiographical crap was, her teaching methods were even worse, and they were really bad when she came to class totally unprepared, which was 99.5 percent of the time! And the prepared 0.5 percent?—geez!

One of her favorite ploys on her unprepared days was to announce, as if she had received a lesson plan from the ghost of John Dewey, America's liberal education advocate, that she thought we should have a talent show, which of itself would not have been a bad idea except that if talent were money, we would have been broke. The total talent in our class of twenty-six students amounted to two girls, LaVon and Jackie, caterwauling an insipid Western tune, Petey, who fashioned himself a terpsichorean whiz, jumping around at the front of the classroom, and some moron whose name escapes me, doing impersonations of Edward G. Robinson ("All right, you mugs!"), Jimmy Gagney ("uh huh, you dirty rats!"), and an impression of Donald Duck that sounded like someone attempting to extricate a popcorn kernel from his throat. Interspersed between "acts," Miss G. would lay some of her Southern corn on us. The class kiss-ups thought it was a marvelous way to spend fifty-five minutes; I thought it was a complete waste of time and, much to Miss Gilstrap's displeasure, I said so.

The "talent" show was a weekly event, usually happening on Friday, a day when our illustrious mentor seemed least prepared; however, her being prepared was almost as bad as when she was not. For example, one day, having recently returned to school from Easter vacation, we entered room twelve to find the walls taken up with large art class tables. On the tables were rolls of butcher paper and scissors. My immediate thought was that Miss Gilstrap had eaten too many chocolate bunnies over the holiday. She announced that we, the entire class, were going to pair up, each duo required to depict on the paper provided a particular phase of travel. Yikes! She must have washed the chocolate bunnies down with heavy doses of moonshine swill! The kiss-ups thought the idea grand; I thought it was a far better idea than having to listen to LaVon and Jackie's rendition of "Little Joe the Wrangler." Halfway through the project, I was praying for a quick return to watching Petey's heavy-footed buck and wing or whatever it was he called it.

But deducing there was no way out of doing the assignment, I quickly teamed myself with Marvin, a kid with a real flair for art, a guy who kids with real smarts allied themselves when an art project was due, knowing that with Marvin's abilities they were guaranteed an "A." As a kid barely able to draw a straight line with the aid of a ruler, I figured I'd need all the help I could get. But with my brains and Marvin's Scripto pen set, the two of us stood to benefit. Was I in for a surprise! Marvin proved a bigger fuckup than me!

I needed little encouragement when Marvin suggested that we choose as our subject early travel in California, which meant horse, mule, donkey, or ox cart; we, rather Marvin, chose the latter for reasons that very soon became evident. With Miss G's approval of subjects, we turned to our tasks with all the fervor of Michelangelo painting the ceiling of the Sistine Chapel, the only difference being we weren't lying on our backs. Marvin with but a few swipes with his number 2 pencil had cart, yoke, and a team of oxen roughed out. But what was this? Square wheels!? It was a stroke of genius bound to drive Miss G into a state of apoplexy; however, it would also guarantee the two of us a hasty trip to the principal's office. But what the hell, it would be well worth the paddling we'd receive to see Miss G-string (a sobriquet accorded her early in the term) lose that Southern genteelness of which she was so proud.

Having revealed his plan to me, and not wanting to tip our hand too soon (the project was scheduled for a two-week stint), Marvin erased the squares that were to pass for wheels, and with a diabolical glint in his eye, set about the task of providing dimension to our roughed-out primitive vehicle and its two-oxen power package.

Smug we were, Marvin and I, barely able to hold in check our delightful thoughts of the wrath soon to be unleashed when our knavery was discovered. Two weeks turned into three, three into four as we erased and retraced our "objet d'art." But on the fifth week, we were advised to put the finishing touches on our work because "tahmorrah, ah will be 'round to inspect yall's drawin's." During the previous five weeks, we had had few inspections from our illustrious mentor, who was content to sit at her desk reading a *True Confessions* magazine or applying an emery board to her nails. Most members of the class had finished their work in fewer than two days, after which they screwed around, the boys playing grab-ass, the girls gossiping and giggling. But it was typical of Miss Gilstrap to stretch the simplest assignment into one of extreme boredom, which is precisely what this contrivance had been. With me leering over his shoulder, Marvin deftly mounted the square "wheels" onto the cart's axles. It was finished, and, I thought, so were we!

We filed into Room 12 the following day, the kiss-ups barely able to contain their joy at the thought of an anticipated high grade; Marvin and I sauntered smugly to the back wall where our masterpiece lay, facedown, ready for the unsuspecting, jaundiced eye of our postbellum Southern belle.

Making her way around the room, her voice twanging like an untuned banjo string, oozing "ah's," "aha's" with an occasional "Oh, mah" thrown in for good measure, Miss Gilstrap sashayed from project to project as if eyeing a stag line of virile Southern bucks at a Tara Cotillion. In what seemed an eternity, she arrived at our table, questioning why we had chosen to turn our drawing facedown. She discovered our reasoning anon!

Marvin and I each grabbed a corner of the three-foot-by-six-foot butcher paper and ceremoniously unveiled our spurious imitation, each of us standing a few paces to the side in order to afford us a better view when the shit hit the fan—and it did!

We were "wicked reprobates," "scoundrels," "ne'er-do-wells," "scamps," "devil's spawn," undeserving of Miss Gilstrap's excellent instruction. For some inexplicable reason, she neglected to lump the two of us in with William Tecumseh Sherman. "Ah garntee, ya'll gawn be visitin' Mistah Rindone foh mawkin' mah effuts tah teach! In fact, Ah got a good notion to cut me a switch and whale the dickens otta of you boys. Squire wheels, indeed!" She then began to pummel the two of us with her bony fists, her butterfly-like blows thudding a tattoo about our arms and shoulders. "Oh, Miss Gilstrap, do it some more," we cried, our mocking driving her into a state of frenzy, eyes glazed, mouth agape, arms and fists flailing the air and us. Then, as suddenly as her tirade began, it ended, Miss Gilstrap leaning against the table, sobbing, her sparse frame convulsing uncontrollably. I began feeling sorry for the old crow, our nefarious act reduced to no more than a hollow victory.

Marvin and I were summarily dealt with, each of us receiving a five-day suspension; Miss Gilstrap completed the school year, resigned and, as far as I know, was never heard from again, thereby ensuring that future eighth graders would not be subjected to her mind-numbing nonsense.

I often pictured her back in her beloved South, attired in an elegant hoopskirt, seemingly gliding through the revered halls of her ancestral home, whopping her "house niggahs" for "bein' uppity," the specter of that square-wheeled cart haunting her till Judgment Day.

EDUCATIONAL PARIAH

$\mathscr{I}$t was 1973. That morning, I was to receive an award designating me an outstanding high school teacher of humanities. I was informed by the organization making the award that I would be asked to say a few words following the presentation. What would I say, I rhetorically inquired of the bearded face staring at me from the mirror of the bathroom's medicine cabinet. I sure as hell couldn't say, "It was a great fight, Ma, and I won it for you." Neither would it be proper that I state that I had done it for my flag and country, a statement reserved for Hollywood heroes in World War II movies. But I had to say something. Then, like Alice stepping through the looking glass, I found myself transported back in time to the spring of 1941 into a seat in the auditorium of Southwest Junior High where our ninth graders under the musical direction of our music teacher Mrs. Bruce were performing the school's annual springtime operetta.

Mrs. Bruce, an unabashed, non-royalty paying pilferer of selections, libretto and music, from the established works of Romberg, the family Strauss, Victor Herbert, and any other composers whose works she could modify to suit her needs, had for the 1941 production titled *El Bandido* and had taken all the music from Romberg's *The Student Prince*; unfortunately, she had given the responsibility of writing the libretto to two of the most dreamy-assed girls in school whose storyline was nonexistent. But worse yet, the star, the bandit, a sort of hybrid of Zorro and The Cisco Kid, was one of the most hated bastards in school, a guy who was forever reminding us peasants that his ancestors descended from English royalty. In many respects, he was telling the truth: He was pompous, a liar, a cheat, and a bully, and we all would have been very willing to crown him. He also considered himself a singer, loud, yes, a singer, no!

Anyway the entire student body was required to attend, and, we were warned, to enjoy while at the same time exercising our best behavior, a tall order considering none of us was too happy to be forced into sitting through three acts of stupid music, sung by the likes of King David and a cast of tone-deaf morons. Besides it was one of the warmest spring afternoons I had ever experienced, the mercury hovering at a click over ninety-five degrees. Yet despite the discomfort, we were herded into the auditorium, a facility without air-conditioning, where the temperature stood a good five degrees warmer than it was outside. Geez, I thought, I hadn't even reached my seat, and I was sweating; worse yet, the heat was softening the Big Nut Chew candy bar stowed in my left breast pocket. Defying the principal's mandate forbidding the bringing of any food or drink to the performance, I had purchased the bar at lunch, placed it in my pocket for future attention, namely after the auditorium lights had dimmed.

Seated next to me was Jimmy, a cocky kid from below the border; his parents owned much ranch land east of Tijuana, making them fairly well-heeled, a fact that Jimmy was always quick to remind those of us less fortunate whelps. Anyway, I did not like him, which made my being seated next to him a tenuous situation.

Halfway through the performance, I decided to unveil my treat. The damned thing had been reduced to a mass of melted goo, making its unwrapping a challenge, the warm chocolate having detached itself from the bar's caramel base. But at last, with all my fingers bathed in a sticky coating, I was ready for my first bite, while on stage, David had begun his first solo. As he raised his voice, I raised my candy bar, anxious for the first bite. It was at precisely that moment that Jim chose to push the melted confection into my face, his action smearing chocolate goo from my forehead to my chin.

Dropping the bar to the floor, I stood up and took a swing at Jimmy missing him and hitting Bill who was seated in the adjoining chair. All hell broke loose, punches flailing the darkened auditorium, curses shouted back and forth, and all the while David exercising noblesse oblige in true aristocratic mien kept right on singing his off-key song. The next thing I remember was Mr. Clarence Harris hauling me and Jim out of the auditorium in the grip of his bearlike paws. David and the ensemble missed nary a beat as we two malefactors were unceremoniously dragged into the principal's office and flung into chairs in the outer office. I sneaked a glance at Jim whose left nostril sported a trickle of blood; my face, smeared as it was with chocolate, resembled a minstrel show's end man. We both squirmed uncomfortably under the jaundiced gaze of the principal's secretary, our uneasiness turning quickly to terror as we heard the inner office's door open and close.

"Send in Jimmy, Miss Nye," the unmistakable voice of Mr. Rindone commanded. Miss Nye nodded at Jimmy, who made for the inner office door, his thick cord trousers making the unmistakable swishing sound commonly associated with the raised wales of corduroy pants. He entered, closed the door, leaving me to ponder my fate which was swift in coming. Jimmy exited the office in record time, a shit-eating grin aimed my way. I knew I was in trouble.

Seated across the desk from Mr. Rindone, I searched his face for some little sign that he was going to be merciful in dealing with me. No such luck! "Jack," he officiously bellowed, "you have been a problem from the first day you entered this school, and your conduct this afternoon only confirms my initial impression of you. Not only are you a discipline problem but you are a poor student as well." Well, I thought, the old bastard has covered all the bases. But he wasn't finished with me. "I see little hope of your advancing to the ninth grade. In fact, I can picture your classmates waving good-bye to you at semester's end," a remark that damned near sent me into fits of laughter.

Exiting the mirror, I knew what I was going to say at the presentation. Following an acknowledgment of my students and the role each of them had played in molding me into a passable teacher, I made the decision to mention Mr. Rindone and the impetus he had provided me more than thirty years before. And though I hadn't seen him in all those years, he was, during the course of my education and eventual entry into the field of secondary education, the invisible agent prodding my recalcitrant self to attend college and become a teacher if for no other reason than to prove him an ignorant man.

Despite its early hour, the breakfast was well attended by San Diego's teaching fraternity. After presentation of the awards, each recipient paid the obligatory respects to those persons responsible for having recommended the recipients for the award. My award was the last presented. The plaque firmly grasped in hand, I made for the speaker's rostrum, gathered my thoughts, cleared my throat, and damned near gagged as I spotted seated in the front row of chairs—Mr. Rindone!

Mind you, it had been more than thirty years since I had seen him or he me. But there he was, his hair slicked back just as it had been in 1941, still sporting those cheap-assed wire-framed glasses . . . "and I especially want to thank a man who thirty-two years past told me that I would never amount to a thing, that I was doomed to failure. That man is seated here this morning, unaware of the role he played in my being honored today. "Ladies and Gentlemen, I give you Mr. Joseph Rindone, my junior high school principal." It took a few seconds before it registered that paying homage to him was the little bastard for whom he had predicted such an unpromising future more than a quarter of a century before.

Suddenly his face lit up, a grin breaking his normally tight-lipped mouth. Standing up, he quickly made for the speaker's rostrum, hand extended. "Jack," he blurted, "not even in my wildest dreams would I ever have predicted that you would become a teacher, and an award-winning one at that. I had you pegged for reform school when you were fourteen." Then, putting his arm around my shoulders, he unabashedly said, "Your success makes me very happy, makes my year!"

Bidding him good-bye, I smugly made my way toward the auditorium exit, self-righteously stretched to my full nine foot nine inches, pride oozing from all pores.

An' Rabbits, George?

---

*L*ouis always reminded me of Lenny in Steinbeck's *Of Mice and Men*: ox-strong and stupid. Louis's family lived on a local dairy where Louis's father was employed. One of Louis's favorite pastimes was to invite some of us dimwits to the dairy where he would proceed to grip a sick calf's nose in his oversize mitt, squashing the poor little doggie's nose to a pulp; another of his favorite tricks was to sit on a knoll next to his house and scare shit out of us kids playing in a vacant lot by firing at us with his .22-caliber rifle. We'd scream and run like hell while Louis convulsed in laughter.

A psycho at age fourteen, we knew better than to get on his wrong side for fear that he would beat the hell out of us or worse kill us; we, the guys in my group, curried his favor by buying him ice cream, surrendering our lunches to him, laughing at his lame jokes, or just plain kissing his ass. We never knew what nefarious action lay behind his ever-present shit-eating grin, and we weren't anxious to be on its receiving end. And we never let on to the aroma emitted from his seldom bathed, fetid-smelling body, always careful to avoid standing downwind when talking to him. When we took showers after gym class, Louis could usually be found ensconced behind the wood shop classroom inhaling a Domino cigarette. And though we disliked him, Louis had one redeeming quality that we all admired—he hated David, our pseudo-aristocrat, master-of-the-dance, off-key singer, brownnoser, blowhard, and self-styled expert on boxing. (After all, wasn't the Marquis de Queensberry an English noble?). We were all in hopes that one day Louis would take it upon himself to beat the tar out of David and in the process break his patrician snoot.

About midway through the first semester, our hopes reached fruition. David made the mistake of questioning Louis's lack of gray cells, comparing them to the brainpower of an amoeba. None of us for one moment believed that Louis knew what an amoeba was, but to him it sounded bad; therefore, he threatened to kick David's butt, the entire matter coming to a head the next week in Miss Gilstrap's class when David, having taken leave of his senses, nasally repeated his accusation. (David always snorted through his nose when voicing opinions.) The next thing we knew, Louis punched David in the mouth, cutting his lip, blood running down his chin from the laceration. David, in his best impersonation of James J. Corbett, began bobbing and weaving as he backpedaled toward the front of the classroom.

The classroom was pure bedlam, desks toppling, girls screaming, boys encouraging Louis to "kick the bastard's ass." Miss Gilstrap, late as usual obviously attracted by the noise coming from her room, burst through the main door just as Louis unloaded a roundhouse at David who backing against the blackboard, managed to duck. Louis's fist hit the slate with a sickening thud, the blow repositioning, the knuckles of his hand about two inches, the blackboard cracked. Miss Gilstrap fainted or being a Southern belle swooned. One of the class kiss-ups ran across the hall to Mr. Harris's room to get help, and he promptly removed the two pugilists to the principal's office. David's lip was swollen, and he was dewy-eyed; Louis's right hand looked deformed, and he was smiling. We, my buddies and I, were wide-eyed, the crack in the blackboard bearing mute testimony to Louis's strength.

Louis and David had one more fight that school year, a bout arranged by Mr. Harris, who theorized that the bad blood between the aristocrat and the moron could only be terminated with a victory by one or the other guys. Because Louis's fist was a long-time healing, the match did not take place until the beginning of the second semester. The fight, spectatorless, save for two coaches and the principal, was to be held in the school auditorium; both pugilists were to wear boxing gloves. My pals and I were pissed; we wanted more than anything, including a chance to look down Miss Gray's blouse at her brace of apples, (she taught journalism to the unlettered), to be able to sit in on the fisticuffs. Bill came up with the solution to our problem.

The fight was scheduled an hour after school was dismissed, and all the students, save for four reprobates atop the auditorium's roof peering through the transom, had gone home. Wrestling mats formed the "ring," stools situation at two of the corners. Louis was dressed in his everyday shorts while David sported what we took to be real boxing trunks (we were later to discover they were basketball shorts he had borrowed from his brother, a former roundball player at San Diego State College.) We heard Coach Mahoney giving instructions to both guys. "Three-minute rounds, a whistle serving as a gong." David sat in his corner snorting as usual, while across the "ring" Louis grunted and pounded his gloves together. The whistle blew, and round one began. It was short-lived.

David came out feinting and snorting, his footwork resembling his lightness of foot on the dance floor; Louis, charging off his stool like an enraged bull, met David in mid-ring with a punch practically delivered off the floor, the blow landing on our blue blood's chin, knocking him "ass-over-tea-kettle." The fight was over, David on his ass out cold—end of fight. When at long last brought back to consciousness, David cried "foul," claiming that Louis had not observed the Marquis de Queensberry rules of boxing. Louis had won, and David never again referred to Louis as a "single-celled organism."

For the remainder of the school year, we willingly shared our lunches with Louis, endured his malodorous stench, and even managed to laugh at his lame jokes; however, we refused his invitations to the dairy to watch as he reduced calves' noses to pulp.

SHE WALKS IN BEAUTY
(WITH ANOTHER GUY)

She walks in beauty, like the night Of cloudless climes and starry skies;
And all that best of dark and bright Meet in her aspect and her eyes:
Thus mellowed to that tender light Which Heaven to gaudy day denies.

—Lord Byron

She was thirteen; I was fourteen. She sat at the piano a few half notes from my station in the percussion section of the junior high school orchestra. Never having experienced love symptoms, I thought perhaps I had contracted a debilitating malady, one common to the adolescent. Normally possessed of a wolfish appetite, I found myself at evening meals, picking at my food, refusing dessert. I became inert, unable to chase down the routine fly ball. In bed at night, sleep came only after hours of tossing and turning, and then it was fitful at best, morning finding me tired and out of sorts. My friends who usually took great delight in my hare-brained acts began to think that I had "gone straight," and that never more would they be witness to my classroom tomfoolery, which though it made them laugh usually resulted in my being led by the ear to the principal's office. My grandmother began to worry about my health, hieing herself to church to light candles for the return of my well-being. Smitten I was!

Though I had known her for some years, her brother and I being close buddies, I had always considered her a pest, a girl younger than I who always seemed intent to screw up some enterprise that her brother and I had concocted. Not unlike my own sister, she was a spindle-legged pain-in-the-ass with no redeeming physical qualities. Seemingly forever dedicated to dogging us, we were constantly chasing her skinny ass home. But that was yesterday.

Today, I stood at my snare drum snatching furtive glances at the nymph seated at the Baldwin. Gone were the pigtails, the dental braces, the flat chest, replaced by flowing auburn tresses, beautiful straight teeth, and a peasant blouse housing heaving boobs. Occasionally she returned my leers with a knowing smile that wreaked havoc with my drumrolls, eliciting the wrath of our teacher/conductor, who threatened to demote me to keeping time on the bass drum. Seeking her acceptance, I composed copious poems to her beauty and its effect on me; at school lunch period, I plied her with ice cream, I, more often than not doing without. I began to bathe every night, scrubbing myself to a point that I literally shone. I ate so many Fleishmann's Yeast cubes I became blotted (Fleishmann's was recommended for ridding oneself of acne). I saved my lawn-mowing money so that I could afford to take her roller-skating at Skateland in San Diego. I kissed up to her brother (although we were great buddies) hoping that he would put in a good word for me. In the end, all was for naught; she had the hots for another.

Alas, all those looks that I had taken as intended for me weren't—she had batted her lashes for the bass drummer, a dolt whose only job was to keep time, boom, boom, boom. I rationalized her fascination with the asshole stemmed from his sporting new cords, while I, because of the lack of coin in our family, was obliged to wear the hand-me-downs of a cousin who lived in Los Angeles and was five years my senior. Sure my grandmother took them in, but in doing so both back pockets abutted each other, creating what seemed one large pocket on my very large bum.

I was heartbroken! I went into a funk, cursing the Fates who had toyed with my emotions. A bass drummer, indeed, a cretin. Aside from his brand-new cords, what did he have that I didn't? Sure he was a good three inches taller than I was; sure he had the build of a young Adonis; sure he had nary a blotch on his handsome face and sure his father was a well-heeled dairy farmer. But hell, his boom, boom, boom, couldn't hold a candle to my exquisite drumrolls.

Convinced she soon would realize her indiscretion and come to her senses, I exercised every ploy I could conceive, short of shoving "Boom Boom's" head through his drum, to assist her in coming to her senses, the awful truth belting me between the eyes the day I espied Boom Boom carrying the coquette's books in his right hand, his left arm embracing her slender waist, as he pompously escorted her to the school bus. Frailty, thy name is woman! But in the words of fellow Scot Robert Burns:

> The best laid schemes 0' mice an' men (or snare drummers), Gang aft a-gley, An' lea'e us nought but grief an' pain For promis'd joy!

Old Bobby must have had my ilk in mind when he penned these lines.

ATHLETIC LONGSHOT

*A*lthough I have over the years enjoyed some athletic success, the one event that stands head and shoulders above the other occurred when I was an eighth grader at Southwest Junior High. As a high schooler, I earned letters in various sports, but the award I always cherished above all the others was a six-inch, green and white "S" I won in track in the spring of 1941, an athletic letter that according to the smart money at school I had little or no chance of winning. But I had an ace in the hole no one at school knew about, especially smart-assed Red Ballard, the eighth grade shot put champ, who had waxed my butt the previous year and, who as captain of one of the eighth grade touch football squads, had not selected me to receive a letter even though I could out punt his sorry ass. I was not enamored of Red, nor he of me.

My hole card was Sebastian Arguello, a shot-putter of some fame at Sweetwater High School. Our neighbor, "Subby," had on occasion run herd on me during the absence of my grandparents and aunts. I had quite quickly grown very fond of him, a handsome, athletic young man. He had always a kind word for me even though at times I tried his patience with my childish tomfoolery.

The success of my plan to dethrone shot put king Red at the annual spring track and field meet hinged on my being able to enlist Subby's assistance in teaching me the finer points of putting. He graciously consented to be my coach provided I was willing to put in the time. To kick king Red's ass, I was prepared to work overtime. We began training three weeks prior to the meet.

Subby borrowed a ten-pound shot from the SUHI athletic department. Ten pounds! Jeez, I had difficulty hoisting the eight-pound shot used in our meets. But as I was to discover, there was method in my friend's madness. He chalked out a ring in my backyard, placing distance arcs at five-foot intervals. He drilled me in form and delivery until I had developed fairly good speed across the ring as well as a passable put. All too quickly meet day arrived. Was I ready for Red? He, the cocky bastard, did not consider me a threat, casting aspersions in my direction as we warmed up. He had a lock on the event, and no one was going to thwart his chances of a repeat of the previous year's win especially a rotund, spindle-legged dope like me.

After two puts by the seven contestants, Red, a smug grin on his freckled face, led, a heave of thirty-six feet six inches outdistancing the field. Last put, it was now or never. I was experiencing the definite hollow feeling of defeat; my last chance to win a coveted letter seemingly about to slip away (again!). Final put—smug-assed Red waived his final try, satisfyingly announcing that he wouldn't need another. The titled event was in the bag. Then a hole was discovered in his bag—me.

Stepping into the circle for my final attempt, my first two having fallen a foot short of Red's best, his "in the bag" toss, I concentrated as best I could on Subby's instructions. Standing at the end line of the ring, cradling the shot behind my ear and in the hollow of my shoulder, balancing it on the tips of my fingers and thumb, coiling my 135-pound body, I shot across the ring, shifted my body in a smooth pivot, and pushed that damned iron ball past my ear, extending my skinny arm to its complete length, snapping the shot off my fingertips into a beautiful arc, the projectile landing with a muffled dirt spewing thud thirty-eight feet away. I had defeated Red and in the process earned the coveted monogram. Ever the "good" loser, Red snorted something to the effect that had it not been for his having a sore finger, he would have buried me. Sore finger my eye; the only sore he had was a sore ass.

I recall with warmth our end of the school term awards assembly and being called to the stage by our coach Mahoney who presented my letter and a very warm handshake. The "S" symbolized not so much that I had bested a boy I detested, but more importantly, it marked the first time in junior high school that I had been recognized for having done something positive. As I accepted the award and handshake, I was bursting with pride.

Sebastian Arguello, my mentor? In 1943, he was killed with the entire crew of an Eighth Air Force B-24 while on a raid over Nazi Germany.

BEWARE THE GREEKS' BEARING

*I*n early summer 1941, my grandmother broke her hip. She was fifty-five years old, in an age when a broken hip at that age meant an extended stay in the hospital. To compound the situation, we were on relief assistance, which meant that she would have to be hospitalized in San Diego's County Hospital, an institution noted for its large wards, understaffed doctors and nurses, and an almost complete disregard for the needs of its patients. She was admitted to County (as the natives called it) where surgery was performed, leaving one of her legs shorter than the other; she was to spend the remainder of 1941 in the hospital until her release three months into 1942, giving rise to yet another problem—what to do with my sister and me while she recuperated.

Although we had an aunt Eveline living in San Diego, she and her husband and two small boys were living in rather cramped quarters in Linda Vista, the newly constructed Federal housing community established to handle the great influx of people coming to San Diego to work in the aircraft industry. She was forced to turn us away, leaving us with but one option, my aunt and uncle in Madera, California. They had but one child, my aunt pregnant with a second, but they also had a large house that could accommodate us. So one June morning, my sister and I boarded a Greyhound bus and headed for the San Joaquin Valley where we would live until our grandmother's release.

Life in Madera was not all skittles and beer. My slave-driving, parsimonious uncle worked my fifteen-year-old ass off in temperatures that at times exceeded hundred degrees, and when the ass-breaking work was completed, refused to pay me what he had promised. The work—I'm not talking about lawn mowing, dandelion picking, or any other chores generally associated with a fifteen-year-old. I'm talking about real work, man's work: digging ditches, mixing concrete (this was an era before a large truck delivered a few yards of premixed), where I was obliged to throw, with a large square-nosed shovel, the ingredients of sand, gravel, and cement matrix into the maw of a concrete mixer, wheel-barreling that mixture to waiting framework for watering troughs, floor slabs, and fence posits. The promised princely sum of thirty-five cents per hour, I collected nary a cent, my uncle claiming poverty.

One of our many jobs during that summer was building watering troughs for the cows on a diary owned by a Greek rumored to be as tight as O'Reilly's balls and the owner of one of Madera's greasy-spoon restaurants. For nine to ten hours a day under a blazing sun, I mixed, wheeled, and dumped load after load of cement to locations all over the dairy, sometimes having to wheel the loaded wheelbarrow fifty to seventy-five yards from the mixer. By day's end, I was one worn-out youngster, happy just be able to pull myself into bed and get a little rest before the routine began the next day, a scenario that went on for five weeks at which time we picked up our tools and mixing machine and headed to the Greek's beanery to collect our wages; I estimated that I had *earned* almost twenty dollars, considering I had also put a few hours on Saturdays. With the money, I planned to buy football shoes in case I made the frosh football team at Madera High School. The football shoes would set me back about six bucks, leaving me a little cash for some school clothes. You've heard of the best laid schemes? Burns's poem was my biography.

Arriving at George the Greeks, we took a stool at the counter, at which time my uncle handed his bill to the Greek.

"Vas dis?" The Greek was questioning something on the bill.

"That's the kid's wages," retorted Uncle Henry.

"I no gonna pay moany to no keed," countered the Greek, gruffly. My uncle, ever the candy-ass, offered not a word in my defense; he just stood there, the gutless bastard I had always branded him. "That's OK, George, just give him a hamburger and a soda." Five weeks of busting my ass, and all I had to show for it was a greasy hamburger and a tepid cola.

Uncle Henry died in 1989; I hope his ass is roasting in hell—in the cubicle right next to George the Greek.

Football? I practiced in sneakers until our coach discovered I could punt hell out of the ball; he got the town banker to buy me some cleats.

THE AWAKENING

A bastard is the son of no one or rather the son of all.

*U*ntil the fall of 1941, I had always considered Everett Long my natural father; however, on a typically hot and humid day in September of that year, the truth concerning my breeding suddenly spewed forth, in ugly vindictiveness, from the lips of the one person I cherished more than any other living being—my beloved aunt Mary Alice. And it had been the result of my fourteen-year-old mulishness in refusing to do yard work prescribed by an uncle-in-law more iniquitous than Dickens's Uriah Heep, a real "Mr. Do-You-Wrong."

It began quite innocently that day in early June 1941, when my half sister and I were placed aboard a Greyhound bus in San Diego and sent to live with our aunt and uncle in Madera, a small agricultural town in Central California, our departure the result of our grandmother having been hospitalized with a broken hip and unable to care for the two of us. Not only had we been offered shelter and sustenance but there was also the promise of a paying job awaiting me. To a fourteen-year-old, the prospect of earning money was an exhilarating thought; even before I had put in one day's work, I had mentally spent half my summer's wages: football shoes, school clothes, movies. But although the work materialized (in spades), my dreams of affluence were destined never to reach fruition, foiled by a cheeseparing uncle-in-law who saw in me the means of lining his own coffers.

I've detailed my summer employment as a mixer of concrete in the previous chapter and the subsequent screwing I took from my uncle and the Greek restaurant owner; however, it was yet another act of trickery on my uncle's part that led to the blowup that apprised me of my base-born background.

My uncle, not satisfied with my working eight to ten hours a day under a blazing sun, decided that I could best serve the financial wants of his family were he to acquire me additional employment. He didn't have to look too far. Situated a stone's throw from the Greek's dairy was a farm, its large fields sporting lines of stakes to which heavy twine was strung to provide the vines of string beans support as they climbed vertically during their period of growth. Row after row of irrigation ditches resembling the fluting on a Doric column extended the length of a very large field; at one end, a sluice box ran the entire width of the field, drain holes situated at the heads of each irrigation ditch could, with the deployment of a wooden barrier, be manually programmed to irrigate ten rows at a time until such time as all the rows were thoroughly saturated, a process repeated every other day. The catch was that the irrigation, because of the valley's extremely hot days, had to be performed after sunset, continuing into the evening hours until all the rows of beans had been watered.

And that is where I came in, my uncle having convinced the farmer, whose name escapes me, that I was just the lad for the job, hard working and swift of foot; I was never apprised of what I was to be paid but just that I was to be responsible three nights a week to irrigate string beans in two large fields, each field measuring twice the width and twice the length of a football field. So every Monday, Wednesday, and Friday, following my regular stint with the shovel, wheelbarrow, and cement mixer, I would hop the fence adjoining the Greek's spread and begin irrigating just as the last rays of sunshine were disappearing in the west, a scenario extending well into the month of August, at which time the farmer decided, much to my relief, that with the beginning of the school year but a few weeks away, he had best give the watering responsibility to one of his regular hands. Money—I never saw a red cent!

But I am getting ahead of myself. During my stint as Gunga Din to rows and rows of string beans, a vegetable I never could stomach, I devised a system that afforded me much needed rest for a fourteen-year-old body already exhausted from a full day of physical labor.

The wooden barrier in place, restricting water flow to the ten rows previously mentioned, I would race to the end of the field, remove my work boots and socks and lie down, positioning my bare feet in two of the ten ditches and fall asleep, awakened when the water hit my feet some thirty to forty minutes later. I would then jump up, don my boots and socks, and race to the head of the field, diverting the water to yet another ten holes and then would once again race to the field's end, the process repeated until every last bean had had its thirst satiated. Once that was accomplished, usually between 8:30 a.m. and

9:00 a.m., I would tighten down the cock on the hydrant, shutting off the flow of water, and run like hell toward the uncle's 1938 Dodge pickup truck waiting to transport me home where a reheated dinner awaited me, my first food since lunch some eight hours earlier.

One evening the son of a bitch failed to show, forcing me to cover the three miles home via shank's mare. After weeks of this routine, I was more than happy to turn over my duties to the hired man.

A few days later, payday at hand, thoughts of Rawlings lightweight kangaroo hide, football cleats laced snugly to my feet were shattered when the Greek refused to pay for my weeks of labor, and the farmer put off paying me until his crop of beans was picked and sold.

Was I pissed? You are damned right, I was! You can't imagine my embarrassment when I stepped out on the football field that first day of frosh football practice my feet encased in worn-out sneakers; fortunately I had a few skills that didn't go unnoticed by our coach who managed to get me shoes.

Like a festering boil, all my anger came to a head that fall day when I announced I wasn't going to mow any goddamn lawn, and that I wished with all my heart I could join my uncle Don, who was working the race meet at Tanforan racetrack in the San Bruno, California. Then truth reared its ugly head: He wasn't my uncle, and the man I supposed to be my father wasn't; my natural father was living somewhere in Canada. And though I wasn't a future candidate for a scholarship to Harvard, the realization that I was a bastard took but a few seconds to sink in. Crestfallen, I sat in the yard until quite late in the evening, my depression prompted more by the messenger than by the message. As much as I loved my aunt, her cruel revelation and her siding with her asshole husband resulted in a rift lasting until her death. Not only did I lose my childhood innocence but I also lost something more important to me—the only member of our family who up to that time had championed me.

Where in the Hell Is Pearl Harbor?

$\mathcal{W}$ith Christmas but a few weeks distant, my aunt and uncle decided to head south on Highway 99 to Fresno for what little Christmas shopping they could afford. My sister was left at home to care for our cousins, ages four and two months.

One of my dreamer uncle's enterprises was a small lumber and firewood lot on the outskirts of town; I was designated to be in charge of the operation in his absence. It being Sunday, I felt there would be little or no call for lumber or firewood. Therefore, I armed myself with two editions of my favorite magazine, *Daredevil Aces*, a pulp number dealing with the fictional adventures of flyers in World War I.

Dropping me off at the yard, my aunt and uncle bade me good-bye, cautioning me that were anything to happen requiring an adult's advice, I was to go next door to Mr. and Mrs. Ito's grocery and request their assistance. Their son George and I had been teammates on the high school's frosh football team, he a guard and I a wingback; we were also classmates in a few classes. I was very fond of George and his parents; they reminded me of the many Japanese-American friends I had had in junior high school. George's parents were ever generous to the members of the football team. Win or lose, they always graciously treated us to ice cream, candy, and sodas.

The morning sky was overcast, the smell of rain in the air. Time dragged. I made one sale of a half cord of firewood at about 8:30 a.m., then sat in the office, completely bored, the exciting stories in my magazines failing to interest me. I tried rolling a cigarette out of a piece of typewriter paper and some very dry tobacco from a tin of Country Gentleman I found stashed in the desk drawer. But failing to find a means of lighting the damned thing, I threw it into the wastebasket.

My thoughts wandered to what I could expect for Christmas. Certainly not what I had requested—a model kit of the Army Air Force's P-26. Too much money ($2.75). I figured house slippers or worse yet new work boots that would allow me to sock the clock with my uncle (without pay, of course). It all added up to a very bleak Christmas and a bleaker New Year.

Finally out of complete boredom, I sat down at the office's ancient Royal typewriter and began two-fingering a letter to my friend Bill back in San Diego. I recounted my miserly uncle, my classes at school, our frosh team's record. (I fudged a bit when commenting on my role as the team's wingback). Finishing the letter, I glanced at the clock in the window of the gas station across the street: 10:15 a.m., I was putting the finishing touches on the missive, debating whether or not I should spin a few more untruths to impress Bill when George ran into the yard yelling something about Pearl Harbor being bombed. I knew where San Diego Harbor was but Pearl Harbor?

"Come on over to the store, Jack. My dad's got the radio on with news." Locking the office door and snapping the padlock on the front gate, the two of us hightailed into the grocery where Mr. and Mrs. Ito were glued to a Philco perched atop the checkout counter. I needed no urging when Mrs. Ito told me to grab a candy bar and a soft drink; George already had his. There we stood, the four of us, one Caucasian kid and three Japanese Americans listening to reports of how the Japanese had pulled a sneak attack on the island of Oahu in the Hawaiian Islands. "And they said all they desired was peace," snorted Mr. Ito, indignantly.

The next day, the entire school's student body was herded into the gym, the upper classmen seated on the gym floor, the lower classmen in the mezzanine. Talk was rife concerning the attack at Pearl Harbor. "We'll kick those Japanese's asses in a couple of weeks." Then we listened to President Roosevelt's stirring speech about the "day of infamy." So inspired were we that two buddies, George Ito and Art Gomez, and I went to the recruiting office after school and asked to be "signed up," a request drawing a loud guffaw from the sergeant in charge. "You boys are a bit young now, but you'll be eligible in a few years." A few years? The damned war would be over in a few weeks, and we'd miss all the action. Jesus, we were naive.

Poor George ended up with his parents at the Topaz internment camp in Utah. In 1943, George, a nisei, was accepted as an army volunteer. I have it on good authority that he ended up fighting in Italy with the nisei 442nd Regiment, one of the most highly decorated outfits in service during the war. Art was killed in France. A paratrooper in the 82nd Airborne, he was killed on D-day. Me, I lucked out. Enlisting in the USAAF in 1944, my ass was probably spared because of a number of freak incidents. I was set back in my gunnery school training by a bad case of what I thought were hives (the medical name escapes me, but it sounded like pitasses rosea); then my grandmother became seriously ill, and I was sent home on emergency leave. I was undergoing flexible gunnery training in Indian Springs, Nevada, when the atomic bombs devastated Hiroshima and Nagasaki. They say that God looks out for the ignorant. Well? The Korean "police action" came later, but that is another story in a different time.

ALL THAT GLISTENS IS NOT GOLD

*1*943—America's involvement in World War II was in its second year, and the nation's war industries were not only employing women in the production of war materials but also, beginning in mid-1942, hiring thousands of teenagers to fill those positions essential to the defeat of Nazi Germany and its Axis partners, Italy and Japan. So it was that about midway through June of that year that my Irish buddy, Joe Dougherty, and I decided that our contribution to the war effort would best be served felling pine trees in the lush forests of Northern California.

Shunning the deafening din of the aircraft assembly line, the two of us opted to spend our time that summer in the quietude promised in the lumber camp town of Westwood, California, where, garbed in lumberjack duds, we would not only be paid princely sums for our labors, but we would also be afforded the opportunity of honing our bodies into shape for the upcoming high school football season; we both envisioned our hardened torsos breaking tackles at the line of scrimmage, toppling linebackers like pins in a bowling alley and outsprinting defensive backs to the goal line. Then, quite unexpectedly, we were tackled short of the end zone!

Having traveled from our homes in San Diego by shank's mare, the educated thumb, and, as far as our slim finances allowed, by Greyhound bus, we arrived in Westwood just as the summer sun was disappearing behind the Sierra peaks, and though it was June, our clothing of T-shirts and Levis provided scant protection from the high-elevation chill that began coating every inch of our ill-clad bodies; in addition, our "bankroll," consisting of the thirty-seven cents I had in my jeans pocket, seemed as unmindful of our plight as did the wind's increasing chill that was beginning to numb the tips of our fingers, our noses, and our ears. But the sign affixed to the hiring office's bulletin board chilled us to the bone:

Brush Haulers Wanted $1.65 per hour Must Be 18 Years Of Age.

Eighteen?! I was four months shy of seventeen, while friend Joe had only recently turned fifteen. Now what? Oh, I forgot to mention that it was Sunday, and the entire village was shut down for the Sabbath. Here we were, two smart-assed teenagers stranded hundreds of miles from the glittering lights of Reno, Nevada, (the biggest little city in the world) where the last leg of our journey had begun earlier that day, and now it seemed that we were destined to return to that gambling mecca by any means available, meaning that we would have to hitchhike or, as the evening's chill increased, freeze off our collective balls. We did a quick about-face and headed for State Highway 38, a cattle path at best, that led to Highway 395, our route south.

Four hitched rides, one with a flaming homo, (the accepted term for funny fellas at the time), who kept referring to Joe, seated next to the guy, as a "real cute kid." I, after noticing the guy was wearing a heliotrope shirt, highlighted by a bright orange four-in-hand tie, seated myself as close as I could get to the passenger-side door; the last hitch was in a produce truck loaded with onions put us in Reno at a little past midnight, the temperature in the low forties and seemingly falling.

Not having eaten so much as a crust of bread since a lunch of store-bought baloney and cheese, we were hungry; however, our thirty-seven cents seemed hardly enough to feed one of us let alone two. Spotting an all-night grocery, a rarity in the 1940s, we and our "bankroll" soon parted company. That is, all but seven cents of it, the quarter spent on a two pack of Hostess cupcakes (fifteen cents) and two cups of coffee (five cents each) which, much to the store's proprietor's distress, we laced with heaping spoons full of sugar and a seemingly (at least to the proprietor) endless stream of condensed milk right out of the can.

Our late-night snack completed, we once again hit the sidewalk into the blast of a teeth-chilling wind blowing down from the Sierra's myriad canyons, our skimpy duds providing us no protection. I felt like kicking myself in the ass for having left my letterman's sweater at home. But necessity being the mother of invention, my brain was hatching a plan that would provide the two of us with enough cash for lodging, food, and bus tickets back to San Francisco where Joe's grandfather lived.

Every moviegoer in the 1930s and 1940s had sat through countless movies in which women from all parts of the United States annually trekked to Reno for quickie divorces, and in all these movies the women, having been granted said divorces, followed the custom of walking to the bridge spanning the Truckee River and throwing their engagement and wedding rings from the bridge into the river's swirling waters. Most women I reckoned knew little about throwing anything except maybe a hip at an unsuspecting man. And with the exception of my sister, who had an arm like Bob Feller, a woman's throwing form resembled a mother waving good-bye to her Thursday bridge group's members; therefore, I surmised that many of the bands of pledge and marriage had come up short of the river, landing instead along its banks and were even then lying in wait for us to harvest, a veritable mother lode for the taking. Scurrying to the river's edge and without benefit of illumination, we began upending rocks, dredging with freezing fingers through the riverbank's muddy sludge, feverishly seeking the touch of metal that would spell the end to our empty bellies and freezing bodies.

"What in the hell are you two kids doing down there?" Ignoring the voice coming from somewhere across the river, we continued to mine, the tips of our fingers beginning to smart from their contact with the prickly shrubs and shards of glass shrouding the river's bank. "I said, what in the hell are you boys doing down there?" This time, there was a don't-fuck-with-me edge to the challenge. We stopped our burrowing, our four eyes gravitating upward to the other side of the river, where outlined against the feeble glow of a streetlight stood a figure the like I had not seen since my last visit to the San Diego Zoo's gorilla cage. There was, however, one distinct difference between the ape and the guy presently confronting us—the ape wasn't wearing a gold-plated badge.

"Get your sorry asses up here, pronto!" Not even bothering to wash the mud from our hands, we scurried up the bank and into the waiting grasp of one of Reno's finest, albeit one of the city's eldest. Jeez, I thought, this guy must be at least fifty, but when you are still in your teens, anyone over the age of thirty is old. "OK, gents, just exactly what were you doing down there?"

My first thought was to tell him we were fishing, but our lack of fishing tackle would have put a crimp in my story. Joe was so damned scared all he could do was stare at the cop's badge while all the time muttering that his dad, a real Irish alcoholic, was going to kick his sorry ass when he found out we had been pinched; I, on the other hand, planned to rely on my stock bailout ploy, a simple declaration to my Spanish Catholic grandmother that I was planning to enter the seminary and study for the priesthood. That religious snow job never failed to gain forgiveness from Mama Chiquita; you see, when a Spanish family had the good fortune to have one of its children, boy or girl, wear the cloth, as priest or nun, it was thought that the child's commitment to serving Christ guaranteed mother and father a penthouse or at least a suite in heaven. I just knew my ass would be saved, but poor Joe, though a Catholic himself, was scheduled for a different fate once word got back home that the two of us were in stir.

The cop was neither Spanish nor my grandmother, and from the looks of him, he could have been of any faith or none at all, but I knew one thing: His liberal-sized ruddy nose gave indication that he was more than just a social drinker and recalling Joe's termagant father's beet-red beezer, I was not about to risk an ass-kicking; therefore, I decided to come clean in hopes that he would buy into our story. "That's the biggest bunch of crap I have ever heard!"

He proved very understanding, so much for telling the truth. And without so much as "I beg your pardon," he marched us three blocks to the city's jail. Now here's where the story takes an unexpected twist.

Herding us to the local hoosegow, a facility in the Reno of 1943 that consisted of four cells, each cell containing two bunks suspended from the wall by chains, a stainless steel toilet, sans seat, and a stainless steel washbowl, he marched us to the last cell, opened the barred door, threw each of us two blankets, and matter-of-factly asked how we liked our hamburgers! For a moment, neither Joe nor I knew what the hell he was talking about; then, suddenly, it dawned on us that he was offering us something to eat. In unison we both blurted out, "Well done, with onion, pickle, lettuce and tomato, mustard and ketchup." And he continued, "Do you lads like French fries?" Heck, yes, we liked fries! "And what flavor milk shakes would you like?"

"Chocolate, please!"

"Now, lads, you make yourselves to home, and I'll be back in a bit with your eats." And away he went, heading for the jail door and whistling "Just Say that I'm a Friend of Yours," a popular song of the day, and he was gone, the sound of a slamming door announcing to us that he had left, leaving the two of us speechless!

Neither of us had as yet not fully grasped what was going on, feeling a few minutes ago that the two of us were headed for the state's Big House, and here we were in a jail cell, its cell door wide open, safe and warm from the frigid temperature outside, awaiting a policeman's return with more food than either of us had ingested in the past twenty-four hours.

Two hours later, our bellies at the bursting point, snug in our warm jail cell, we settled in for a much needed sleep. The next morning Officer Lyons (we finally asked his name) awakened us at seven o'clock, and after washing the sleep from our eyes, we were walked to a restaurant two blocks from the jail where the good officer treated us to a breakfast of eggs and bacon, a short stack of cakes, biscuits and gravy, and a mug of steaming hot coffee, after which we were escorted to the local Western Union Telegraph Office where Joe sent a collect telegram to his grandfather requesting he send money for two one-way tickets on Greyhound.

Three hours later, the two of us were traveling west on Highway 80 toward San Francisco where each of us got summer jobs, but that's yet another chapter in this memoir. Officer Lyons? After making certain that we were out of harm's way, he bid us good-bye, good luck, and instructed us to keep our noses clean, adding that in all his years on the police force, he had never heard of anyone finding a ring on the banks of the Truckee River. One thing that has always given me cause for reflection is that we never thanked him for his kindness, an oversight that bothers me to this day.

I Left My Tooth in
San Francisco

*A*fter our aborted lumberjack gig and our night in a Reno jail cell, Joe and I headed for San Francisco, thoughts of summer employment in Baghdad by the Bay, dancing in our pea-sized brains, as our Greyhound bus sped westward.

Arriving in downtown Frisco after midnight, we decided that in deference to his advanced years, we wouldn't drop in on Joe's grandfather but would use the remaining few bucks from the money order the old guy had sent us to rent a room for the night in a seedy hotel; we found one some blocks east of Market Street, a decision we both were to regret.

As any citizen of San Francisco knows, the city's southeastern area is landfill, its composition part sand, part goop drawn from the bay; of course, Joe and I, two out-of-town rubes, having no knowledge of this regional information, soon learned to our dismay what that mixture of grit and sludge had in store for us. Our first hint came when we entered our third-storied hotel room that reeked of insect repellant!

Only minutes after we had ensconced ourselves between the sheets and blankets of our shared bed, we sensed we were not the bed's sole occupants. Our legs began to itch, our legs tormented by the crawling and biting of something. Throwing aside the bedclothes revealed the source of our annoyance: legions of bedbugs and fleas hopping and crawling the width and breadth of bed! We spent the rest of the night sleeping on the floor.

Morning found us nursing sore backs and necks, our legs covered in hundreds of reddish welts, all itching like hell! A quick plash of water to our eyes, and we bolted downstairs to the lobby and made for the street, but not after we had flipped off the effete night clerk, and told him to get fucked! Over black coffee and sinkers at a Market Street doughnut shop, while scratching our legs, we mapped out our next move. We decided to hop a streetcar and head for Joe's grandfather's place on Broderick Street.

Grandfather Dougherty, a pipe dangling from his mouth, welcomed us with open arms, introduced us to his landlady, Mrs. Feeney, a corpulent, frumpy old woman, and suggested we look for jobs in the Bay area; and Mrs. Feeney said she would be more than happy to bed and board the two of us (for a price, of course). Now we needed employment, but where to look? Mrs. Feeney, also the neighborhood gossip, had heard that the Longshoreman's Hall at Fort Mason was hiring high school boys to work on the docks for the summer. Next morning, Joe and I made tracks for the hiring hall.

Because I was sixteen, I was hired; Joe, who was fifteen, was not. He eventually got a job in the Nabisco Cracker Company boxing saltines. I was to be paid $1.65 per hour; Joe earned the princely sum of fifty-five cents an hour plus all the crackers he could eat. He, however, worked but an eight-hour day while I labored ten hours, six days a week. I took home, minus union dues and tax deductions, about seventy-five bucks a week; my buddy cleared twenty dollars.

With our landlady gouging each of us seven clams a week for room and board, poor Joe had little to show for his toil, save for pant pockets full of cracker crumbs! I, on the other hand, was salting away in the bank twenty dollars a week; I would have saved more but for my generosity in keeping my young companion financially afloat. So affluent was I I could almost feel those new football cleats on my feet.

Our residency in the house was but a notch above the insect-infested flophouse where we had spent our first night; I slept on a lumpy couch, Joe on a cot in his grandfather's room. For a few weeks, Mrs. Feeney insisted making our lunches, but after one week of sardine and vegetable sandwiches, I begged off, preferring to buy lunch from the numerous lunchrooms located along the waterfront. Joe consumed so many soda crackers he became as rotund as 1940s movie comedian, Lou Costello.

Because of our differing work schedules, Joe and I seldom enjoyed each other's company; I worked ten days straight; he put in five days, a schedule affording him weekends off which he usually spent taking his grandpa to Golden Gate Park and to eight thirty Mass on Sunday morning. I, on the other hand, was more interested in the fine arts, spending many a weekday at the Golden Gate Theater listening to the bands of Count Basie, Harry James, and Erskine Hawkins, often sneaking in an extra show before finally being asked to remove my ass from the theater. On a more serious note, I also availed myself of visits to the many fine museums, especially the Palace of Fine Arts. I even took in a track event at Kezar Stadium where the Swedish runner, Gunder Haig, ran a record-setting 1,500 meters.

But mostly I worked, each morning finding me on the California Street cable car that took me to Van Ness Avenue where I transferred to a bus that transported me to North Point Street and eventually to the Hiring Hall on Mason Street where I lined up to receive my day's assignment on one of the piers that numbered from one to forty-five along the length of the Embarcadero. Each day brought with it a different task for our twelve-teen working crew.

On most days, our work involved unloading boxcars filled with materials essential to the war effort: ammunition, food, parts, and even toilet paper. One day, we would be breaking down a boxcar loaded with thirty-seven millimeter shells in the morning and in the afternoon humping one-hundred-pound sacks of flour onto flats. Occasionally, we carried officers' gear into the holds of transport ships where we were subjected to all sorts of bullshit from GIs shipping out to war zones, most of the cracks questioning our manhood, "How come you aren't in, you fuckin' asshole," or "What are you, chickenshit?" We kept our mouths shut, opting to ignore the taunts and just going about our business. But tougher than the cracks were the thoughts that many of the grunts making us feel like shit would probably be killed on some Jap-infested island. My grandma's refusal to grant me permission to enlist in the marines made the verbal abuse all the more unbearable. But on my return to San Diego in September, I would once again present her my case. But that's another story.

Our boss's name was Bill Heinz, a real honest-to-goodness son of a bitch, a frigging slave driver, a tyrant having little patience with our crew; while other supers allowed their charges a few extra minutes for lunch or more than one break during our ten-hour shifts, Heinz would ride our asses even while we were eating a sandwich during lunch, resulting in many of us suffering from indigestion. His favorite expression was, "Let's hump it!" But for some reason, we really worked our balls off for the guy. Perhaps it was pride, or perhaps we wished to prove to the prick that we weren't "fuck-offs."

In any case, we were always the first crew to wrap up an assignment for which we never received so much as a "Good job, Boys." But the truth behind his kick-ass supervision was revealed to us a few days before our summer employment was terminated, when another teen-team foreman ambled over to where our crew were unloading a boxcar full of medical stock. "Here's the dough I owe you, Heinz," he rasped through spittle-spewing lips. "Are you planning to split the dough with these kids?" On hearing this, we all froze. What the hell was he talking about? Why would Heinz split anything with us unless it was one of our skulls? "You mean you ain't told 'em," chided the foreman.

"Told us what?" queried Jim Eagan, a broad-shouldered fullback from St. Ignatius High School.

"Why, hell, lads," retorted the double-gutted foreman, "he and me has had side bets goin' all summer on whose crew could break down loads faster." Jim shot a look at Heinz that would have melted a glacier; Heinz, his mouth twisted in a shit-eating grin, muttered something totally unintelligible like "umphing," and "humphing," like Major Hoople of the comics.

After a minute or two of hemming and hawing, he admitted to his having taken advantage of us, his alibi being that he was going to use his winnings to throw us a big seafood supper on Fisherman's Wharf on our last day of work. His announcement managed to smooth our ruffled feathers, not so our muscular Irish football player. Jim countered Heinz's announced intention with a scurrilously phrased retort, something he hadn't learned from the Jesuits, "Listen, you old bastard, if you are just blowing smoke up our asses, I'm going to toss your skinny Jewish ass in the bay!"

The next afternoon, Heinz not only bought us supper but also picked up the tab at Joe DiMaggio's Restaurant, no fish and chips joint. We ordered anything we wanted from the bill of fare, appetizer, entrée, and dessert. Heinz, drunk as a boiled owl, short of falling on his knees, "ashked ush" to forgive him his "dishonesty" in failing to let us in on his little game. We did, all except Jim, who steadfastly held to his conviction that our boss was a cheap Charlie, a lox jock. About nine o'clock, we left Jolting Joe's, shook hands all around (even Heinz's), said we'd see each "next summer," and head home. I never saw them again.

Oh, before I close this episode, I had better explain this chapter's title. Perhaps, if you happen to be a fan of boxing, you may have heard of the 1899 Battle on the Barge, a pugilistic contest between Jim Corbett and Joe Choynski, the match held on a grain barge in San Francisco Bay in 1899, attended by a crowd of 257. Corbett was declared the winner after twenty-eight rounds; conversely, a fight of lesser note was fought in 1943 on San Francisco Bay inside a boxcar on Pier 43 between two teenagers, both boys part of a twelve-man crew assigned the task of unloading boxcars loaded with war supplies; unlike the Corbett-Choynski bout, the match lasted but five minutes.

I had been working with Heinz's crew for about a month when a new guy joined us. His name was Manny, a senior at Lowell High School. Because of his habit of breaking into supplies intended for service men in the South Pacific, he continually pissed off our crew; the son of a bitch was without conscience. Although the rest of us weren't angels, we got our dander up when it came to consideration of guys our age fighting the Japs. Whenever one of us would criticize his depriving a GI of something—cigarettes, K rations, fruit juice—Manny's stock reply was, "Fuck the stupid bastards for going into the service. The schmucks knew what they were getting into."

One day, it was about quitting time, Manny, seated on a crate in the back of the boxcar, was sucking back on a can of pineapple juice. I asked him if he ever thought about the GI, sweaty and thirsty in the humid insect-infested island jungles. Unfazed by my patriotic remark, he continued quaffing the juice; enraged by his indifference, I slapped the can out of his hand. "Get off your ass, you bastard," I yelled contemptuously; wiping his mouth with his shirt cuff, he slid off his perched atop the crates, shot me a smirk of defiance, and unleashed a roundhouse punch to my jaw that knocked me on my ass; also, the punch managed to knock out one of my teeth. The fight was over. I sat on the boxcar floor, blood oozing from my mouth, my tooth nestled in the hollow of my hand. The fight was the last one I ever had, but I remember it as if it happened yesterday. I have no way of knowing whether or not he ever entered the military, but I am certain of one thing: I pity the poor Jap or Kraut who gave him any shit. He was a tough bastard; also, I hope, if he did enter service and had occasion to open a crate of food supplies, he found half of its contents missing.

MOVE OVER DANTE

*F*rom the time my grandfather presented me with a milk cow, six rabbits (five does and one buck), I have had the responsibility of a job since I was eight. In many cases some jobs were more demanding than others, but, nonetheless, jobs in which I was to accept responsibility and accountability, moral decisions with which I often found myself at odds for one reason or another. In an earlier chapter, I recounted the summer of 1941 in which my parsimonious uncle screwed me out of wages I had earned, busting my fourteen-year-old-ass in the oppressive heat of California's Central Valley; I will, therefore, not rehash that nightmare, but deal, instead, with some of the other employment I managed to procure or jobs that were procured for me by relatives who firmly believed that work, any type of work, made the man (and kept Grandma Bowman in Kool brand cigarettes).

Solar Aircraft Corp, fall of 1942—I had just turned sixteen, and my family's failure to enlist me into the United States Navy (I was turned down because of marginal color blindness) left them with another mouth to feed; they were not happy. So-o-o-o, I was urged to find a job that would allow me to pay my way.

World War II had depleted the male workforce in the United States, and San Diego was no exception; the region's aircraft plants and shipyards, desperate for workers, were forced to hire not only women but high schoolers as well. Hundreds of teenaged boys, those over sixteen years of age, joined adults on the assembly lines of Consolidated Aircraft; others worked in the many factories that manufactured parts for B-24s bombers and PBY patrol aircraft. I worked at Solar Aircraft shaping manifolds for those aircraft, receiving the princely sum of sixty cents per hour for a twenty-three-hour workweek.

Dante's *Inferno* had nothing on Solar; hot, noisy and filthy, oppressive, cacophonous, discordant noise brought back memories of the spiritual chalk talks Father Ryan gave his parishioners about hell at Sunday Mass, sermons right out of Part I of the *Inferno!* Any movie studio looking for a location to film the classic epic could have found none better than the interiors of the buildings housing Solar Aircraft's workforce; Dante's nine levels of hell had nothing on Solar's building number two; all that was needed was the ice of the ninth circle and the three-headed Lucifer enjoying a snack on Brutus, Cassius, and Judas Iscariot. Occasionally, a bloodcurdling scream from a drop hammer operator, whose foot inadvertently released the machine's ponderous hammer, divesting the man of a limb, hand or arm, cleaved the building's fetid, unventilated air, a bloodcurdling scream guaranteed to scare the shit out of you! I hated the place so much that I was always on the lookout for another job, any kind of job; the opportunity presented itself in the person of my floor foreman, Arky, a toothless clodhopper from Arkansas, who, having taken a dislike for me, took it upon himself to get me fired!

The cretin's displeasure with me was spawned one Saturday at lunch when he told us he'd done "right" poorly on an IQ test administered by the company psychologist but that he planned to study and take the test again and score higher. I saw my opening: "You dumbshit," I snickered and added, "you can't improve your IQ score by studying, because IQ tests determine your intelligence, your capacity for reasoning, for understanding, and for similar forms of mental activity." I had him by the balls!

"You sumbitch!" he snorted, "You and your two-bit words are goin' ta get ya a pink slip!" He was a man of his word.

Monday afternoon, a slip of paper affixed to my time card directed me to report to the employment office. I did and was unceremoniously sacked! The reason—my whistling, while pounding manifolds into shape, was annoying other workers, resulting in a reduction of production. Guess who filed the complaint? Yep, the simple-minded rube with the deep-as-the-well IQ. A quick trip to the payroll office, and I was headed for the bus stop on Pacific Highway, my hand firmly clutching a severance check and five twenty-five dollar war bonds. I felt like Dante exiting the abysmal environs of purgatory into heaven's celestial milieu.

Thus ended my first real job, employment for which I received Social Security credit, a job in which I was obliged to use a time card, a job where I received compensation in the form of a check, and the first job from which I was sacked. From that day in early 1943, until I entered the armed forces, my jobs, with the exception of my summer on the San Francisco docks in 1943, my employment consisted of a hodgepodge of tasks including doughnut glazer, bowling alley pinsetter, restaurant busboy and dishwasher, theater marquee changer, a job I obtained because I could spell better than the average teen. Oh, less I forget, I also had a stint working in the receiving section of a downtown

San Diego department store where I unloaded and counted the dishware contents of shipping barrels, a "position" for which I received the princely sum of thirty-five cents an hour. My future appeared very bleak, a condition that lasted way into my early twenties. I was on a treadmill of failure. My last odd job as a teen was painting, after a fashion, my girlfriend's parents' house, a task for which I was woefully unqualified, a project so botched up the young lady and her parents never spoke to me again.

Dear Mr. Soon-to-Be-Eighteen

$\mathscr{I}$t was the spring of 1944, and having reached my seventeenth year, the previous October, I began receiving with great regularity letters from the marines and the navy urging me to enlist before my eighteenth birthday and avoid being drafted into the army. Born in a navy town, the thought of being an anchor-cranker appealed little to me; however, the thought of me parading around my neighborhood in Marine dress blues seemed just the ticket. I was also damned sick of high school, its teaching staff, and the saddle-shoe-shod blue bloods from San Diego's Kensington district.

Jumping on a number eleven streetcar, I hied myself downtown to the Marine Corps' recruiting office, with visions of close order drill, weekend passes, monthly visits to the paymaster caroming like a three-cushioned billiard shot off the walls of my teenaged skull, each thought was punctuated by the metallic clacking of the streetcar's wheels on the steel rails. I could already envision myself, rifle at the ready, storming a beach on some remote island in the South Pacific. I would come home to San Diego a decorated hero, seated atop the backseat of a staff car, waving acknowledgment to thousands of San Diegans lining both sides of Broadway, cheering their boy-hero home. Then, quite suddenly, my dream of coming home, the conquering hero, burst, exploding into a thousand shards a few days later by a highly decorated, ramrod-straight marine topkick.

Having survived the rigorous, at times embarrassing, physical, a three-hour ordeal in which I was obliged to parade around in the buff, while navy medics peered and probed into every aperture of my seventeen-year-old body, I returned to the downtown enlistment office where I was ordered by a pimply-faced corporal to line up with the other "grunts," his voice ringing with the timbre of a neutered Pekinese and not a devil dog, that is until he did an about-face, revealing a tunic festooned with two rows of ribbons; quite suddenly, I felt like a neutered Peke!

After what seemed an eternity, I stood facing "Old Ramrod," his craggy face perusing a sheaf of papers held in his catcher's mitt-sized hands, his Marine-green encased elbows resting on the table, so many stripes, bars, and ribbons on his uniform, I wondered were he to receive another stripe, bar, or ribbon, where in the hell would he put it. The man looked as if he had just stepped out of a recruiting poster.

Wishing to please him and to show him that I had the stuff to be a marine, I stood at attention, at least I stood at what I considered to be attention. Still his war-wearied eyes scanned the papers, seemingly oblivious to my presence. Finally, he looked up, his chiseled jaw clenching and unclenching. "Son, we can't use you in the Corps. You're color-blind." My reply, laced with what today would be considered politically incorrect, was, "What's color-blind have to do with shooting slant-eyed Japs!"

The sergeant, quick to sense my disappointment, retorted, unkindly, I might add, "There's the army." That remark really tied the rag to the bush. The army? Hell, didn't this guy realize that I was trying to become a marine because I didn't want to be a dogface? But not having forgotten my Virginia-bred grandfather's lectures about good manners being the mark of a civilized gentleman, I thanked him, did an about-face, retreating for the door and onto the sidewalk dampened by a light April shower, my thoughts of epic heroism seemingly as worthless as the refuse being swept into the street's storm drains.

Crestfallen, I trudged across lower Broadway, making for the streetcar stop, grappling with the specter of sober reality: Having been refused enlistment, I now faced the indignity of admitting my failure to the neighborhood's lunkheads, who collectively had scoffed when I announced my plans of enlisting. But perhaps more annoying was the thought that I would have to return to school and the numbing and dumbing of the classroom.

The return trip on the number eleven, bereft of the promise relished on the trip downtown, seemed never-ending. Not only was I in a funk but also worried and uneasy that all my braggadocio of a few weeks past would only lend credence to the scuttlebutt that I was all wind and piss and as popular as a baked ham at a Jewish wedding reception.

With the wounds of derision festering still, I grudgingly returned to Herbert Hoover High School, my first stop at the attendance office where I was summarily meted out ten hours of after-school detention for having ditched the previous week.

It was back to the classroom and the annoying nasalization of Miss Hutchinson, the school's junior lit teacher, whose approach to instruction rivaled that of the infamous Mary Gilstrap in its ineffectiveness. She could take a poem by Robert Frost and make it sound like the instructions for feeding the family cat; feeding the family feline would have proved more educational and certainly more rewarding, especially for the cat. So it was back into her class of silly "read-arounds," half the guys in the class reading at about the sixth-grade level when they agreed to read, the silly-assed girls reading as though they were the descendants of Sarah Bernhardt, all flailing arms and inflated inflections, each girl trying her damnedest to "Out Herod, Herod." As for me, I attempted to merely blend into the background, parking my ass behind all 220 pounds of the "cardinal's all-city tackle," whose mass provided more concealment than a well-constructed duck blind.

But Miss H., not hoodwinked by my well-laid scheme not only asked that I read for the class but that I also stay after class, at which time she informed me that her grade book showed that I owed her two book reports and that if not submitted within a week would result in third quarter failure. My first thought was how I was going to submit two reports when my reading material since the first of the year had been limited to magazines *Esquire* and *Sunshine* and *Health*, the latter a monthly published by a nudist organization, my interest limited to ogling pictures of nude female types playing volleyball, shuffleboard, or merely striking suggestive poses as they lolled around the compound's swimming pool. *Esquire?* I seldom ventured beyond Varga's scantily clad, leggy, full-bazoomed, perfectly coiffed blonde cuties, swell for adorning the fuselages of American military aircraft but hardly the subjects for a high school book report. Besides, book reports were not my métier.

I was feeling very uncomfortable, and since Miss H. had never taken me to her heart, I sensed she was as gleeful as Torquemada, the Inquisition's grand inquisitor, sending another heretic to the rack. But, of course, she had reasons to dislike me. As class smart-ass, I was the spilled ink on her grade book; in truth, she would have been well within her rights had she insisted I be expelled, but this thought is the offspring of hindsight and the contrite thoughts of a man about to enter his seventy-fifth year. But back to the belated book reports.

I spent the better part of an afternoon writing the reports, both deliciously bogus, spurious hybrids culled from the stories I had read in pulp magazines, each paper religiously in complete compliance with the criteria demanded by Miss H.: titles, authors, dates of publication, publishing houses, genre, story summaries and critiques, double-spaced, properly margined, also writer's name, class, and date dutifully noted in the upper right-hand corner, all neatly ensconced within the covers of an overpriced folder. Finished! Now all that was left to do was submit the "reports." Done! No questions, merely blind acceptance.

The results? Four days later, both fakes returned, a grade of "A" on each, plus comments—"Well done, however, I am not familiar with the author." I felt like an artist who had passed off as genuine as a bogus Renoir; I also felt that it was time to pull stakes, to leave what I considered a very uninspiring and unproductive situation. I quit, just cleaned out my gym locker, and made for the bus stop on El Cajon Boulevard, dirty socks and gym trunks in hand, on the way informing a teacher on campus security that he could "kiss my ass."

Two weeks later, with an affidavit in my paw signed by my grandmother stating that I had her permission, I enlisted in the U. S. Army. It hadn't been difficult convincing Grandma that the signing of the paper would be in her best interests; you see, she had long since given up any hope of my becoming a priest, so she figured that the next best thing would be receiving an allotment check each month. Though her decision would not gain her admittance into heaven, it did guarantee her a steady supply of Kool filter cigarettes. Granny was a real pragmatist.

PS: Had my dreams of becoming a marine been realized, I might well have taken a Japanese bullet on Iwo Jima!

I Was a Teenage Shill

*A*s Bob Ryan, his felt fedora set rakishly on his balding pate, headed for the billiard parlor's doorway, both his arms pinned securely in the grasp of two San Diego PD Bunco Squad plainclothesmen, he turned to me and in his rich Hibernian brogue stated matter-of-fact that he would return in a few hours and if I would keep an eye on the place until then—and he was gone, onto the sidewalk, into the black-and-white, and off to police headquarters. Mr. Ryan, the owner and operator of the Adams Avenue Billiard Parlor, was also the local bookie; if you wanted to place a bet on a horse, he was your man, his sideline having netted him numerous trips downtown. His pool hall, merely a front, lent an air of respectability to his operation. It was early 1944.

Having quit high school halfway through the second semester of my junior year and awaiting induction into the United States Army, I was experiencing difficulty obtaining any sort of employment. Early one morning, I wandered into the billiard parlor, in hopes of honing my skills as a snooker player. Mr. Ryan, reading glasses firmly seated on the bulbous tip of his very prominent nose, was intently scanning the day's scratch sheet. "Mornin' Johnny. Lovely day, isn't it?" The sour odor of sacramental wine on his breath told me he had that morning attended Mass at St. Didicus parish, a daily ritual since his wife's health began failing some years past. Folding his racing form, he planted his elbows on the glass top of the cigar case behind which he was sitting, and peering over the top rims of his glasses, asked, "Your dear mother, she's Spanish, isn't she?" I acknowledged she was.

"Can you speak the language, Johnny?" Yes, I could and could read and write it as well.

"Jesus, Mary, and Joseph, you're just what I'm in need of!" I was completely lost; however, Mr. Ryan quickly apprised me of his "need," and it wasn't Spanish lessons he was seeking.

During World War II, the Federal Communication Office placed numerous restrictions on what could and could not be aired. One victim of the office's mandate was the transmitting over the airwaves the results of horse races on the East Coast and Midwest (there was no West Coast racing for the duration). The only radio station providing track results was XEMO, located in Tijuana. As regular as clockwork, it provided win, place, and show data, including not only the names of the tracks, horses, jockeys, trainers, and stables but more importantly the payoffs—*in Spanish*! Enter bilingual Johnny Bowman, teenage shill. Out of work and damned near penniless, I quickly embraced Mr. Ryan's proposal.

All that was required of me was a few hours in the late morning and early afternoon at which time, pencil and paper at hand, I would sit behind the counter translating into English the results of races and payoffs at America's major tracks as well as those from Mexico City's Hippodromo de Mexico, a second-class track noted for its rigged races. Compensation? Fifteen dollars (American) per day, unlimited use of the establishment's pool tables, all the sandwiches, candy, and soft drinks I could consume plus the envy of all my ne'er-do-well sidekicks. My head turned by the recompense offered, I gave little thought to consequences, one being that I could be arrested as an accessory in Mr. R's bookie operation. But fifteen bucks and all the tempting residuals? In the patois of my second tongue, I was no "pendejo," or stupid shit! Elated, I quickly accepted the offer but on the condition that my job would not require the donning of a felt fedora.

My initial two weeks went swimmingly. I needed only to record results Monday through Saturday, giving me Sunday to completely blow my fifteen smackers, a wastrel supporting those ne'er-do-wells who envied me; then on Monday it was back to my stool, radio, pencil, and paper, religiously decoding results for the two-dollar betters who frequented the pool hall. And every Monday morning, Mr. R asked the same question, "Did you receive the sacraments yesterday, Johnny?" His concern for my soul always followed by, "The first race at Narragansett Park will be on in a minute. Copy the results accurately, my boy." And so it went for twelve workdays; the thirteenth brought with it change in the extreme.

Lucky thirteen! The morning had given way to early afternoon; I was on a roll, flawlessly recording one result after another, my brain a veritable decoding machine. Engrossed in the task at hand, my teeth working on a Baby Ruth candy bar, I failed to notice the two men, each attired in rumpled clothes, slithering through the pool hall's door. "What the hell are you doing" spewed the shorter of the two, his spittle spraying me, the counter, my worksheet, and what was left of my candy bar. My first thought was to tell him to shove it, but noticing the San Diego PD badge pinned to his vest, I refrained; also, I noticed Mr. R, in the grip of the taller guy, being escorted toward the door. "Oh, I'm a junior at Hoover High, and our instructor encourages us to listen to Mexican radio stations and to practice translating Spanish into English. She says it's the only way to learn the language." I was thankful he didn't request the teacher's name; true, I had attended HHHS but had never taken a Spanish class. My canard had worked, the cop none the wiser. I breathed a sigh of relief as the three exited, assuring Mr. R that I would indeed take care of business. Securing a fresh Baby Ruth from the candy case, I jotted down the results of the fifth race at Florida's Hialeah Park, "La carrera terceda en la pista de carreras Hialeah. El ganador, Jung (Young) Gwooman (Woman) Pagando ocho dolares, etc., etc., etc . . ."

True to his word, Mr. Ryan returned in a couple of hours, none the worse for his experience; after all, he was a regular downtown. Me? I continued translating until orders arrived from the military directing me to report to Fort MacArthur for induction, ending my career as a bookie's shill and probably saving me a trip downtown to the pokey.

It was while I was undergoing air force basic training in Texas that I learned of Mr. Ryan's wife's death, the old man following her a few weeks later. It is during my trips to the Communion rail that my mind wanders back to the precious days spent with my spiritual advisor.

"Did you receive the Sacraments, Johnny?"

"Yes, Mr. Ryan, I did, and every time I do, I think of you and include you in my prayers."

WHO ARE YOU, DICK TRACY?

*W*ell, after hours of creating five solid, well-written paragraphs and then losing them to the whims of this damned machine, I am about to begin all over again, hoping that I don't mistakenly hit a wrong key and wipe out every frigging thought, word, and phrase. In the words of Shakespeare's Henry V, "Once more unto the breach . . . !" If I lose this round, I will, after I have dispatched this accursed instrument with my 20-gauge shotgun, commit suicide, Roman style, by falling on the tip of my ball-point pen. But I digress.

It was the spring of 1944; World War II was in full swing. In the Pacific, the marine corps, at great loss of life, was laying claim to Japanese-held Pacific Islands. In the ETO (European Theater of Operations), the invasion of Fortress Europe was in the planning.

Stages, while on the home front, and specifically in the local communities constituting the environs of San Diego, California, four soon-to-be GIs were in the planning stages of an operation guaranteed to afford each of them fame bordering legend; on the other hand, their parents would be branded pariahs, neighborhood outcasts no longer welcome at church bingo parties, ostracized from weekly coffee klatches, assiduously branded the parents of four devils' spawn, and ignored by clerks while shopping at the local A and P. We were the four hooligans: Dave, Rudy, Joe, and I.

With time dragging, our military orders pending, we four miscreants decided that we would leave the old neighborhood some one thing to remember us by, some one thing that would turn our neighbors loathing of us into unbridled repugnance. Being young and stupid, we gave little thought to the legacy we would be foisting upon our parents; matter of fact, none of us gave much thought to anything or to anyone, each of us figuring he'd be killed anyway, so we refused to stew over the consequences of our plan. We had done some shitty things, but this caper was going to be the shittiest of them all! The thought of it had all of us drooling. It held promise of rivaling the actions of Mrs. O'Leary's cow. We would set a fire across El Cajon Boulevard, the much-traveled artery connecting downtown San Diego with La Mesa, the crown jewel of the foothills. The devilment was afoot!

The logistics, save for one important detail, were established very quickly: two dependable cars, one five-gallon can of gasoline, a box of kitchen matches, and, that important detail, an airtight alibi, an item demanding our undivided attention. We quickly surmised that what we needed was someone to vouch for our whereabouts within the time frame that the dastardly deed was being executed.

We all agreed there was one logical choice upon whom we could rely: Sunny, a carhop at Keith's drive-in located three blocks from the site of our prank. A middle-aged woman, age had failed to diminish her beauty, her curvaceous body the subject of many a teenaged boy's dreams; there wasn't one of us who had not mentally ravished her. However, we all respected her, never being smart-assed or disrespectful when she waited on us at the drive-in. She was ever willing to take short money for a check we couldn't cover and not place us in an embarrassing position when we were with a girl as was a favorite pastime with some of the other carhops, who always seemed ready to make you feel like a cheap son of a bitch. "Keep the change? No, you can use the three cents more than I can." Sunny was above that sort of shit. Sunny was always willing to make you feel proud and the girl with you willing to go on another date with you. "Thanks for the tip, sport. See you later and don't do anything I wouldn't do." Always sensing that we felt a little awkward in the company of a girl, she never failed to praise us whether it was for a new sport shirt, an exceptionally good crew cut, or merely the color of our eyes. So a few evenings later, we headed for the drive-in, confidence a passenger in the backseat of Rudy's 1936 Ford sedan.

Pulling into an open parking slot, we signaled to our confidant. Spotting us, she strolled toward us, nodding at the occupants in cars as she moved, a smile tipping the corners of her mouth. "What'll it be, sports?" she asked, her voice velvet-edged and strong. Rudy's chop-topped car required she bend from the waist to see into the car's interior, providing all of us a peek at her substantial boobs. But we weren't there to lasciviously ogle tits, so we got right to it. Sunny's reaction was not what we expected; in fact, we were, in the words of William Shakespeare, "quite chapfallen."

"You're going to do what?!" she questioned, her mouth thinning with displeasure, too surprised to do more than nod. Then in a velvet-edged voice, she spoke to all four of us, "Don't do it, sports. Old Smooth-Britches Howard will arrest all your skinny asses, take you downtown, and book you, canceling out your enlistments." Howard was a local cop who rode around on a three-wheel motorcycle during the day, chalking automobile tires, and writing tickets for parking infractions. Some times, he had the evening duty, cruising the streets in our neighborhood in a black-and-white and giving teenagers a bad time; he hated kids, and he especially disliked the four of us. We were responsible for nicknaming him Smooth-Britches because the ass end of his uniform pants supported a sheen, the result of his planting his large ass on the leather seat of his three-wheeler. Unlike some of the members of the San Diego Police Department, too old for military service, Howard was of draft age, but for some reason he had never been called up. We all figured he was a queer. Anyway, despite Sunny's admonitions and her promise to back us when questioned about our whereabouts on the night set for our deviltry, we forged ahead, determination etched on each of our blemished faces.

Two nights later found us in Rudy's brother's 1934 DeSoto sedan, parked on Illinois Street, on the south side of El Cajon Boulevard, full gas can at the ready, Rudy behind the wheel, me riding shotgun, Joe in the backseat behind the driver, and Dave, matches in his mouth, gas can at the ready, seated behind me. Traffic was light, foot traffic almost nil. While awaiting the right moment to cross the boulevard, I suddenly felt a foreboding that something unpleasant was going to happen; I was damned near proved correct!

During the war, shoes were rationed, but the government's edict of two pair of shoes per citizen per year fazed San Diego's teens naught. Quite early in the world conflict, enterprising high school students found the answer to the shortage of footwear fifteen miles south of San Diego, across the international border in Tijuana in the numerous stores, whose owners made a good living fleecing American tourists and military personnel dumb enough to cross the border into Baja California, the Gyrene, feeling that he had screwed the Mexican out of his original asking price for a "solid silver" ID bracelet, discovering a few days later the "silver" as green as the scum on a farm pond, and that it was he who had been screwed!

But back to the footwear. Called *huaraches*, the sandals were inexpensive, had most styles, of which there were a half-dozen or so sold for about five bucks for an American; however, those of us who spoke the Spanish patois of T-Town could usually shave a few dollars off the asking price. I could and did! The sandals, fetid to the olfactory sense, were constructed of uncured cowhide, the soles about an inch-and-a-half thick to which we wise guys affixed metal taps that announced our coming long before we arrived; however, there was one problem associated with our "calling cards": In attempting a quick getaway, they offered little if any traction, resulting, at times, our slipping and doing a spread eagle on the sidewalk or pavement, leaving our faces, hands, and arms lacerated and bleeding. And who was the guy in our bunch who prided himself on all the taps he had nailed to the soles of his Mexican scoots? Dave! His sandals damned near did us all in!

We, like Henry V's English forces at Agincourt, awaited "like greyhounds in the slips, straining upon the start" (Shakespeare's *King Henry V*, act 3 sc. 1. You see, I wasn't always asleep in my high school English class). In the parlance of the day, "we were hot to trot." And trot we did, straight across the boulevard, Dave holding the gas can out the car's back door, laying down a liquid swath from south to north. Then once we were a half block removed from deposited petrol, Dave, matches at the ready, leaped from the car's back door, raced back to the gas-covered pavement, struck, and tossed a handful of matches into the gas, and turning, sprinted back toward Rudy's car, slipping at arm's length from the open door of the car. During the turning, sprinting, striking, and tossing, I had slid from my position behind Rudy across the backseat to the door through which Dave had exited. Lucky for him, I had. Grabbing Dave's outstretched arm, I yelled for Rudy to move, the car taking off, dragging poor Dave's scrawny body down Illinois Street, the taps on his huarache's soles shooting sparks in every direction.

Finally, after what seemed forever, Rudy stopped the car a couple blocks from the scene of the crime, where we retrieved a shaken and unnerved Dave, his face ashen, his profanity still intact. "You bastards were going to leave me, weren't you?" he bellowed, saliva forming at the corners of his mouth. Assuring him that abandoning him was the furthest thing from our collective minds, we got him into the car and raced toward Adams Avenue and our second car. Abandoning our odoriferous jalopy, we quickly piled into our get-away buggy and made for the drive-in, Dave, by now having regained his composure, urging Rudy to "Get this fuckin' crate to Keith's. I want to see the shit I've done!"

Nonchalantly pulling into the eatery, amid the sounds of fire trucks' wailing sirens filling the night and setting off the howling of dogs in the vicinity, we spotted Howard's big, shiny ass, a perplexed look on his face, making the rounds of vehicles parked in the drive-in's service slots. Quickly exiting our car, we all raced to the sidewalk to witness what was happening four blocks away. East and west, traffic on the boulevard was at a standstill; billowing smoke from the fire corkscrewed into the air. Firemen, their fire hoses shooting great streams of water at the conflagration, seemed moving at a snail's pace. We, on the other hand, jackasses that we were, were convulsed with braying but not too loud for fear that Howard would hear and have no further need of questioning those folks who sat in their cars dining on cheeseburgers, French fries, and root beers. Finally our curiosity sated, we hustled back to the car, Joe solo in the backseat, Rudy, Dave, and I in the tuck-and-roll upholstered front seat, Dave seated in the middle. It didn't take long for Howard draw a bead on us, hoist up his drooping uniform trousers, and make a beeline for Rudy's car.

Taking up a position on the passenger side, my side, of the vehicle, hands on hips, one foot on the running board, his chest stuck out like a male prairie chicken's during mating season, Howard cut loose with some of his choice profanities. "Now, you little bastards, where have you been for the past hour, and don't give me any bullshit, you little pricks!"

Joe replied mockingly, "Gee whiz, Mr. Constable, we've been here the past hour drinking highly milk-diluted coffee, paid for with the money we get from turning in soda bottles. We aren't as fortunate as you and your fellow flatfoots who get their java free." At that, all of us found it difficult stifling snickers threatening to explode as Howard glared into the backseat, his bloodshot eyes riveted on Joe, who sat, unconcerned, rotating around in his mouth his ever-present toothpick, while Howard, his mouth resembling the blowhole of a surfacing Pacific gray whale, spewed spittle over Dave and me, his anger barely under control, contemptuously hissing, "Prove it, you smart-asses!"

Convinced we had him by the balls, we invited him to ask Sunny. He did, and the positive nod of our favorite carhop's head told us that we were in the clear; Howard did a quick about-face and quickly marched back to our car, resentment written all over his contorted face. "All right, punks, your girlfriend's saved your asses, why I don't know, but I'll tell you one thing, if it takes forever, I'm goin' to bust all of you," and glaring at Dave, he hissed, "and especially you, you little kike!" Dave, ever the teen-master of repartee, leaned forward, turned toward Howard, a shit-eating grin on his face, and brashly inquired, "Who in the hell are you, Dick Tracy?" I almost pissed my pants!

Howard turned abruptly and headed for his patrol car, got in, kicked over the engine, ground the gears into low, and exited the drive-in, his rear tires screeching. That was the last time I saw Howard, who, having left the police force for a defense job in Detroit, never returned to San Diego. All but one of us returned to San Diego. Joe, who was a crewman on an aircraft carrier in the South Pacific, died of wounds he suffered after a Japanese kamikaze crashed onto the deck of the carrier, our old partner in crime buried at sea. We, the survivors of World War II, returned to the States, Rudy to work as a telephone line repairman in Boise, Idaho, and Dave, after an education at UCLA, to become a successful trial lawyer in Northern California. Me? Wandering from one unskilled job to another, my life was a muddle for more years than I wish to admit, the one really outstanding action in my life was having been involved in the infamous El Cajon Boulevard conflagration; it was years before I managed to straighten out my life and that was accomplished only with the assistance and encouragement of many loving folks; more on this later.

IV

The Fifties

BUT FOR THE GRACE OF MAC

$\mathcal{M}$ac was the most civilized person with whom I had ever had the good fortune to be associated—honest, considerate, caring, unprejudiced, and totally tolerant; he was also black, a condition that never seemed important to those of us who shared his unconditional friendship. It was my good fortune to have been taken under his wing in the spring of 1954 when the two of us worked together at a San Diego lumber company, he a truck driver, I a yard flunky, he a college graduate, I a high school dropout, whose life had up to this point had been in an extreme state of flux: I was like the rudderless ship drifting aimlessly, bereft of a charted course. It was Mac who supplied me with my change of bearing, Mac who through sheer persistence pointed me in the right direction.

Ferman McPhatter, a graduate of San Diego State College, an outstanding and honored two-sport athlete for the "Aztecs," had long dreamed of becoming a high school coach; however, following the awarding of his degree, he soon discovered that prejudice was not limited to States where the citizenries language was punctuated by Confederate yells, pickup trucks flying the Stars and Bars from their radio antennas, and using the word "nigger" in more instances than Mark Twain employed the term in *Huckleberry Finn*. It seemed that San Diegans were very willing to cheer Mac's prowess as a receiver on the SDSC football team and as an excellent high jumper of the school's track and field squad, but his application for a teaching/coaching position in the city's school system was rejected; yesteryear's cheers had become today's jeers. It appeared that racism was alive and well even in the sunny climes of Southern California. On a brighter note, the San Diego Unified school System's loss proved my gain and my salvation.

For weeks during the spring and summer of 1954, Mac had been on my ass! "Go to junior college, John. Take some night courses!" He meant well, but, shit, I was taking in over a hundred a week, had a nice little Chevy BelAire, coupe, a closet full of fashionable clothes, and a girlfriend. Why in the hell did I need to attend school? In my mind, I was doing all right, but in Mac's mind, I was frittering away my life, and, good friend that he was, he was concerned. I had on occasion, while the two of us were delivering a load of lumber to some construction site, or jawing during lunch, talked about my lack of education and not having completed my junior year of high school, but never did I broach the subject of returning to school, denying that I had any regret of having left school and certainly not expressing a desire to attend college, two year or four year.

But despite my negation to the idea of my returning to school, Mac, his conversations seldom devoid of some reference to my education, with seeming obligation, continued his sales pitch with the tenacity of a college football coach attempting to sign a blue-chip high school athlete; the man simply refused to give up on me! Finally, after weeks of his lectures, I gave in. Fed up with his hectoring, I agreed to take a night class at San Diego Junior College in the fall.

Spring quickly turned into summer, and promises to attend night classes were soon forgotten in all quarters save one—Mac. Quite innocently, I felt the issue had been laid to rest; Mac, however, had another idea that manifested itself the second week of August.

In the yard, filling an order of 4 × 6s and 2 × 4s, Mac, offhandedly, asked, "When are you planning to go downtown and enroll?" His remark resulted in my dropping one end of a 4 × 6 on my foot. Ever the bullshit artist, I quickly countered with, "Thursday night, Mac." But what I considered a masterful deception proved a house of cards as Mac requested I pick him up at his home on my way downtown. I wasn't very bright, but I was smarter than a box of rocks, it taking but a few seconds to figure out his motive, and it wasn't just a ride in my cool, two-toned Chevy.

Thursday evening found me standing in an enrollment line, awaiting my turn to sign up for an evening class commencing in a week. A few feet removed from the queue, my friend's eyes busily scanned the college catalog, the long, dark index finger of his right hand expeditiously flipping page after page; then, what I had feared all evening came to pass: In his smooth, rich baritone, Mac inquired, "Which class are you enrolling in?"

With the skill of a foot soldier parrying a bayonet thrust, I deftly retorted, "U. S. History 17A."

To which Mac countered, "Which nights?"

I informed him the class met on Monday and Wednesday evenings from "seven till nine." My words had barely cleared my lips when he retorted, "Psych 10 meets on Tuesday and Thursday nights. Take that too." Silently, I cursed him for sticking his nose where it didn't belong, but I had a plan, an ace up my sleeve. I would enroll for both classes, attend a couple of sessions, then, unbeknownst to him, I would drop both classes, and he would never be the wiser; I had not counted on enjoying the learning experience afforded to me by two very competent instructors, teachers who inspired scholarship.

A couple of sessions turned into a couple of weeks; a couple of weeks turned into a month, and so immersed was I in my studies that had if it not been for final exams, the semester would have ended unnoticed. Never, since my sixth grade with Mrs. Mattie Corbett, had I been so utterly happy with learning, thrilled that my life was at long last charting a definite course, my rudderless days seemingly ended. Even the good grades I received in both classes paled in light of my awakening. But so self-centered was I at having completed successfully the courses attempted that I gave only token thought to the real reason for my good fortune—Mac. Though I welcomed his praise, I became truly concerned as his efforts to procure employment continued to fail, failure that dogged him for many years.

Mac's concern for me and my situation remains a constant reminder that any success we achieve in life is not restricted only to our own actions but is in many instances the product of our associations with other humans, whose interest in our well-being takes many forms. My one real regret is that I failed to keep up with Mac, my rationale being that with a family to support and pressing responsibilities at work, I had very little time for socializing, at best a bullshit excuse. No, the real reason was that I was an ingrate.

A few days ago, driving home from a meeting at the university, the part Mac played in shaping my life was vividly presented to me in the figure of a homeless person standing forlornly on a street corner, his unwashed hands holding a cardboard sign on which was scribbled a barely legible sign:

HOMELESS & HUNGRY CAN YOU HELP ME?

Extending my arm out my car window, I shoved a few bills into the man's soiled hand, staring at him as, with dirt-encrusted fingers, he counted the money; at that moment, I experienced a horrifying thought: There, but for the grace of Mac, go I!

PS: February 15, 2009

Yesterday's (Sundays) fish wrap's obituaries' section brought the news of the death of my beloved friend and benefactor. Mac died on January 28, his body giving out after years of wheelchair confinement. Although for years I neglected contacting Mac, our occasional intercourse limited to brief telephone conversations, the memory of the man and the role he played in shaping my life never waned. For Mac there will, as long as I live, be a place for him in the pantheon of my mind, a place located next to Irving Parker and George Gross.

Requiescat in pace, good and loyal friend.

The Lost Sheep
Returns to the Fold

I became a lapsed Catholic somewhere between pre-pubescence and when I began shaving. It wasn't that I had planned it; it just happened. Chalk it up to laziness or refutation of the tenets of the Catholic Church; whatever my reasoning, the day I turned in my cassock and surplice, I turned my back on the organized religion. However, I must have done so with apprehension, for I continued wearing my St. Christopher medal and scapular into adulthood; also, I retained many of my solemn oaths when confronted with anything disagreeable or vexing—"Holy Mother of God," "Jesus, Mary, and Joseph!" and, of course, the blasphemous "Jesus H. Christ!" followed by making the sign of the Cross.

But beyond that, I had not been inside a church since I was sixteen, and then only because I had the "hots" for girl who attended a Catholic school for girls; she, like a Lorelei luring a Rhine river boatman to destruction on a reef, sweet-talked me into attending Christmas midnight Mass; by Boxing Days she had thrown me over for a muscle-bound weight lifter, a moronic tackle on the school's football team. But the "unkindest cut of all" was that my genuflecting and reciting Latin responses during the Mass hadn't rewarded me so much as a good squeeze much less an hour of passionate necking. I deduced that God was not the compassionate Supreme Being I had learned of in my Baltimore Catechism. I, therefore, washed my hands of the Roman Catholic Church, little realizing at the time that the Lord does work in strange and unexpected ways. Jump-start to August 1954.

Mind you, it had been years since I had wet my thumb in holy water, a decade since I had taken God's Body at the Communion rail, but on a Thursday in 1954, as I hurried down Fourth Avenue on my way to Lion's Clothiers to purchase a new tropical worsted suit, I noted streams of people hurrying up the steps of Saint Joseph's Cathedral; stopping an elderly lady, I asked what was going on, why all these folks were entering church on a Thursday afternoon. Her brow drawing together in an agonized expression, she piously replied, "Why, young man, it's the Feast of the Assumption of the Virgin Mary."

Thanking the lady, I turned and made a beeline up the steps and into the church's redolent vestibule, the fragrance of incense immediately conjuring memories of an earlier time, when a very young altar boy, kneeling before an altar, reverently swung a smoking censor upward, its pungent vapors brushing gently a crucifix raised high in the hands of a devout Irish priest. The tinkling of the bells announcing the priest's entry into the sanctuary brought me back to the present; I walked quickly down the center aisle until I came to a half-empty pew, genuflected, crossed myself, and slid in.

To the priest's "In nominee Patris, et Filii, et Spiritus Sancti, Amen. Introibo ad altare Dei," I found myself responding. "Ad Deum qui laetificat juventutem meam." It was almost as if I had never left the church; Once again, attired in cassock and surplice, I knelt on the epistle side of the altar, reading responses in Latin from the Mass card. On the Gospel side, my buddy, Joe, was responding in kind, both of us, two ten-year-olds, spiritually enraptured by the ritual and the role each of us played.

Following the final blessing by the priest, he and the servers exited into the sacristy, the signal for the pews to empty; I remained seated until only the statuary of the Christ, the Virgin Mary, and I were alone, the church silent save for the hiss of tires and engine noises drifting in from the street. I was alone—my company, the saints staring down from the stained glass windows, the fourteen stations of the cross depicting Jesus' swift trial, his crucifixion, and his burial, and the ever lighted votive candles expressing parishioners' vows, wishes, and desires.

Finally, I slid out of the pew, genuflected, crossed myself, and made for the church's massive doors; outside in the late afternoon sun, the parable of the lost sheep kept running through my mind. All I lacked was a "baa" and a woolen suit. That was the day I returned to the flock, never again to stray.

Wedded, my Irish lass, Marion and me (1956)

Dean Irving Parker: "Give me one good reason for admitting you to the College of Men." He was Angel Number Two.

A twenty-eight year-old Frosh, University of San Diego,
College for Men (1956)

USD Football: "You've got a choice, football or me!"
She was s-o-o-o understanding.

"Why don't you be a cheerleader? You've got a big mouth."
And we had been married but two months.

"You do plan on passing my Theology class, don't you?" My first venture in front of the footlights, "Home of the Brave." Bill Franklin is the wounded warrior. Director, Fr. Leo Lanphier, S.J. (my Theology instructor) (1957)

Cast of "Stalag 17." Best Actor Award (1957)

Graduation, University of San Diego, College for Men (1960)

My Third Angel: Professor George Gross

P.A. Voice of the Pacific Coast League San Diego Padres (1961-1971)

Classroom instructor (1961-2003)

Coach: St. Augustine High School Cross Country Squad (1963)

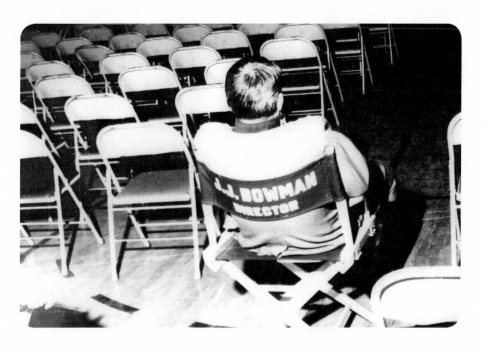

Drama Director: St. Augustine High School

Junior Varsity Football Assistant Coach to Coach Bill Wittaker (1966)

Coach: Jr. Varsity Baseball, Ramona High School (1984)

The Brood: Conway, Bernadette, Eileen, and Molly (1968)

Pa and and Ma: Pa's 50th class reunion, University of San Diego (2010)

DEAN IRVING PARKER:
A MAN FOR ALL REASONS

*B*y May 1956, I had completed two semesters of study at San Diego Junior College and in that eight-month period had completed successfully twelfth units of credit. The world was my oyster or so I thought. My oyster proved without pearl when I received from San Diego State College's Office of Admissions a letter stating that I did not qualify for admission to that institution.

Where could I turn? I couldn't believe that all the nights I had faithfully attended evening classes, at times so tired from a day of filling lumber orders under a blazing sun that I could barely drag myself into the classroom and plant my tired ass in my desk, sleep my constant companion, my eyelids feeling like two counterweights, the thought of transferring to state an invisible finger, prodding me into a state of wakefulness, had been for naught. I felt violated, placing blame upon Mac for his having talked me into abandoning my going-no-where life for what he promised could prove my salvation—education. Education, my ass! All I had for my hours of study were twelve lousy units of credit, a stack of overpriced texts, and wasted hours I might better have spent sitting with a girl in the Sky Room of the El Cortez, downing good Scotch whiskey, nibbling her pink earlobe, and watching airliners passing precariously close to the hotel's top floor.

Now what? Tail between my legs, I returned to the lumber yard, to the derisive comments of the damned work crew, "We warned you that Mac was filling you full of crap. Hell, he went to college and look where it's got him!" Mac! Where was Mac? He wouldn't laugh at my misfortune. True, he didn't laugh, but he gave me the worst ass-chewing I had experienced since air force basic training. No, he didn't laugh, but, over an afterwork glass of suds, and after soothing my bruised ego, he asked, "You're a Roman Catholic, aren't you?" I retorted I was, but what the hell did my religion have to do with my getting an education? He explained that perhaps my salvation lay atop a finger of land jutting out from Kearny Mesa into Mission Valley, once an antiaircraft installation during the early days of World War II, where the Catholic diocese of San Diego was constructing a university that would consist of a college for women and a college for men. "Why don't you apply there, John?"

Hell, why not! Hadn't I been an altar boy when I was a kid? Of course, there was the problem of my having left the church for three decades past, but, on August 15, 1954, on the Feast of the Assumption, I had rejoined the flock. Since then, I had been a seven o'clock Mass regular at St. Martin's in La Mesa and a weekly customer at the post-Mass doughnut and coffee gathering in the parish hall—and had the gut to prove it! The more I gave thought to Mac's proposal, the more I was convinced that I should apply for admission to the college (university status was years away). I had misjudged Mac whose only concern was my welfare.

So, after work one Wednesday, armed with my unofficial transcript and letters of reference from Mac and my boss, Jim Gilchrist, I pointed the nose of my 1953 Chevy northwest, toward the Office of Admissions at the University of San Diego College for Men and an appointment with Irving Parker, the College for Men's Dean of Admissions, and the man, who, along with Mac, would prove my salvation.

Ensconced behind a large, oaken desk, nattily attired in a good-looking tan tropical worsted suit, a blue four-in-hand knotted in a half-Windsor knot securely positioned beneath the wings of a spread collar, sat the dean, stout, spectacled, and all-business.

"So, Mr. Bowman, you are seeking admission to the University of San Diego, College for Men, is that right? I see by your letters of reference that you come highly recommended. However, I also note that you left high school early in the second semester of your junior year, that your grades to that point were average at best, and that following military service, you made no effort to complete your high school studies, and, therefore, you have no high school diploma. Might I ask why?" I thought of telling him that because of war wounds, I was unable to attend classes, but not having been closer to the action than Las Vegas Army Air Force base in Nevada and Seymour Johnson Field in North Carolina, I had second thoughts about taking that route. So I gave him my best hangdog look, hoping it would strike a sympathetic chord in his heart. It didn't!

"Now," he continued, "I have in my hand your official transcript of courses you successfully completed at San Diego Junior College, and I find them most commendable." My breathing improved. "I note that you earned twelve semester credits over a period of one year and that your GPA is a solid 'B'. Of course, twelve credits in night school is hardly a recommendation for admittance into a degree program in a four-year institution. Furthermore, you are lacking high school classes in American government, mathematics, English, and science. In a word, sir, you are the most ill-prepared individual I have interviewed to date!"

As I watched the dean riffling through my papers, I sensed I was screwed. Then, leaning back in his swivel chair, and peering at me over the top of his horn-rimmed glasses, he asked, "And why do you wish admittance to our school?" Quickly dismissing the urge to supplicate myself, I stated simply that I wanted an education. For what seemed to me an eternity, the dean, issuing forth an occasional "um" or "ugh," shuffled and reshuffled my papers with rapt attention to their content, seemingly ingesting and digesting every word. Finally, having deposited the stack of papers on his desk, the dean spoke, "Mr. Bowman, I have decided, in light of your age and the success you have achieved in the classes taken at San Diego Junior College, that, on the strictest probation, I am admitting you to the College for Men commencing in the fall term with this caveat: If at semester's end you do not meet at least 'C' average, you will be summarily dismissed from this college. Do you understand me, Mr. Bowman?" I assured the Dean that I did, and after a few minutes of thanking him and shaking his hand as if it were a water pump handle, I took my leave. I was elated, overjoyed at the thought that in a few weeks I would officially be a member of the 1956 freshmen class; a few weeks into the fall term, I would turn thirty! But what the hell, I was in, albeit on strict probation.

Full of myself, I glided down the administration building's highly polished floor, figuratively patting myself on the back, in a self-congratulatory reverie, that quickly took on the trappings of a nightmare when it suddenly dawned on me that I wasn't the sole reason for my good fortune. No, there was Mac, who not only advised me but also supplied the kick in the ass that led to my enrolling at San Diego Junior College, the individual who patiently prodded me into believing in myself. Then, there was the dean, who, despite his misgivings, admitted me for the first semester of my freshman year but conversely the man who accepted all my reasons for desiring a college education.

Mac? After years of rebuff by the San Diego Department of Education, he became a teacher and an administrator; unfortunately, a horrendous auto accident resulted in his suffering injury to his spinal cord, confining him to life in a wheelchair. He is currently counseling troubled youngsters. Although I have been remiss in keeping in touch with him—I have hundreds of invalid reasons—hardly a day passes that he isn't in my thoughts. The dean? He came very close to requesting I leave school following my having received two "Fs" in my first semester. "Mr. Bowman, didn't I make myself perfectly clear when I stated that you were being accepted on strict academic probation?" I conceded he was correct and that I was ready for the consequences. Removing his glasses, he leaned forward, his elbows on his desk, and looking me straight in the eye, he blurted, "Damn it! How could you fail two classes and do so very well in four others? You flunked logic and math, but you received excellent grades in English literature, American history; speech, and drama." I explained I had no excuse for failing the two classes, my defense based on my inability to figure out syllogisms, and I was at a loss dealing with math problems, which were more complicated than long division. "Remember, Dean, I left high school before I had taken any advanced math courses."

Closely examining my transcript, nervously clicking his ball-point pen, its metallic cacophony cleaving the room's quietude, the dean seemed lost in thought, when suddenly, and without provocation, he stated, "Because of the four good grades, I am willing to give you a second chance, but don't try my patience. You either cut it second semester, or you're finished!" Sensing that he wasn't making idle threats, I promised that my second semester grades would contain no "Fs." Besides, I apprised him; having married a few weeks into the first semester, my wife, also unhappy with my grades, had laid down an ultimatum: Improve your grades, or get back behind the wheel of that lumber truck! Hell, I was now wearing black-and-white saddle shoes and button-down collared oxford cloth shirts; the thought of once again donning dungarees and flannel shirts did not appeal to me. Shit! I was strictly collegiate. (Dean Parker passed away a few years ago, and I was asked to speak at his Memorial Mass; I did so, honored that I had been asked).

DEAR COLLEGE DAYS

Days of Our Youth,
Six Parts Sloe Gin.
One Part Vermouth
(Apologies to Tom Lehrer)

My introduction to college proved a real shocker; for instance, because I dropped out of high school midway through my junior year, I had not taken classes in math beyond algebra, which I flunked in grade nine; fortunately, English and the social sciences proved not a problem as I had been always a voracious reader of literature and history. In fact, thanks to my aunt Mary Alice, who had not only taught me to read when I was nearly five but also provided me a wonderful set of children's books with classic works geared to the young mind, works including Shakespeare's *Merchant of Venice*, Homer's *The Iliad*, the poetry of Wordsworth, Poe, Browning, Whitcomb Riley, and Tennyson, plus the classic epic, *The Song of Roland*, to name but a few; you will recall, I hope, that Mrs. Mattie Corbett had me reading the likes of James Fenimore Cooper while I was a student in her sixth-grade class. All history fascinated me—American (The Wild West); English (The War of the Roses), Greek (The Trojan War), and Roman (Hadrian's Wall).

I was, therefore, despite my lack of computative skills, much better prepared than were my younger classmates, who, despite sporting high school diplomas, encountered great difficulty dealing with the language skills; for instance, one guy thought that a preposition was asking a girl if she would "go all the way." Another bozo, who confused "coma" with "comma," declared as a premed student. And so it went, that first semester. There were, however, some high points that negated the experience of my aborted football stint and my two failed classes first semester.

One of the classes I passed that first semester was theology I, taught by Father Leo Lanphier, a Jesuit priest. I gave little thought to this rotund, well-spoken man of the cloth, until that afternoon when he confronted me while I was sashaying my way to my American History class.

"I need to talk to you, Bowman," he blurted, his corpulent body blocking my way to Room 12.

"Father," I retorted, "I am late for class!" Shunning my pleas, he stated that he was directing a play titled *Home of the Brave* and that there was a role just made for me in the production. "Father, I haven't acted since I played the character of Robinson Crusoe in elementary school," I stated. He quickly countered that it made little or no difference if I had or hadn't acted before. "I'll mold you into a better actor than Darren McGavin," he pontificated, quick to point out that as a member of his theology class, it might prove ill were I to not agree to take on the part.

Once again finding myself between that proverbial rock and a hard spot, I agreed, but only if the padre got my wife's permission; I did not want a repeat of the football mess. I don't know what Irish soft sell he presented Maid Marion, but she agreed. To ensconce the entire episode, not only did I play to perfection the role of the cigar-chomping corporal, but for my performance was, at school year's end, I was awarded the medal for best supporting actor. "Petkins" never missed a performance, sharing the post-performance limelight with me, while I kept insisting that had I remained on the football team she would have been accorded the same treatment. But perhaps the role receiving more accolades was my stint as a cheerleader.

My wife always contended that I was chosen a cheerleader because I had a "big mouth." Whatever the reason, I became one of USD's cheerleading trio, the other two, John Markley and Roger Ralston, establishing a new standard for bawdiness, my yells resulting in being summarily hauled before the college's provost and advised to "clean up my act." Refusing, I was immediately defrocked, my cheerleader sweater committed to the mothballs. The stadium's sideline had seen the last of me, but the theater's stage had not. Exit stage left!

My remaining three years as an undergraduate were kinder and more fulfilling than had been my first year, and, except for "snookums" discovering that I once again was trying to make the varsity football team, I was actually learning and enjoying the educational experience, attributed, perhaps, to one truly exceptional instructor, whose comments on returned composition made my debauched cheers pale by comparison.

His name? Father John Bremner.

Four years in the military had placed me in contact with some dyed-in-the-wool bastards, but until I innocently chose Father Bremner's American Literature class as one of my electives, I had never met a man who better fit the title. Not only did I not think he had a father but I was also damned certain he lacked a mother. He was, in the beginning, the dogshit on the soles of my cordovan wing tips!

I recall my first day in his class. He was throwing questions at us about the works of Henry James and Edith Wharton. Shit, the only James with whom I was familiar was Betty Grable's husband, bandleader, Harry James. Then, just toward the end of class, Father asked if the name F. Scott Fitzgerald held any meaning to us; one asshole, whose name escapes me, blurted out, "She's a black jazz singer."

Hell, I thought Father was going to suffer a stroke; pulling himself together, he walked to one of the windows in our second-story classroom, poked his oversize head out the window, and bellowed at top of his lungs, "I'm surrounded by morons!" His action set the tenor for the remainder of the semester.

An Australian by birth and a product of Catholic education, he could abide neither sloppy spelling, lack of knowledge regarding agreement of subject and verb, nor complete ignorance of punctuating the possessive case, and woe to the student who added an apostrophe to indicate possession to the pronoun "it." Although his American Literature class was instructional, Father's real forte lay in the field of journalism, a fact that some of us with a more masochistic bent discovered second semester when, like mass migrating lemmings bent upon self-destruction, we signed up for his journalism I class.

Journalism I—those of us who had survived American Literature and the turgid prose of Henry James and Edith Wharton were introduced to a new discipline: rough draft, editing, and the rewrite! The slovenly shit we wrote for our other classes was never acceptable in Father B's class. He must have purchased red pens by the carload, our returned papers often resembling the spillage from a severed artery. And the comments, "What's this feculence?" Though a proponent of what he called "our beautiful bastard language," he often let fly with a word that had us scurrying for our Webster's.

He eventually left the priesthood, renouncing his holy orders and marrying; his final teaching position at the University of Kansas where he became Stauffer professor of Journalism. In 1980, the essence of his teaching formed the basis for a fine book titled, *Words on Words, a Dictionary for Writers and Others Who Care about Words*. His fame as a grammarian extended into his being a consultant for numerous newspapers.

In 1985, he went through surgery for bladder cancer; the disease metastasized, taking his life a year later. I recall to this day one of his sayings, "Stick to English so as not to reveal your ignorance of Latin." I could bid him "requiescat in pace," were it not for a premonition that a growl with an Australian accent would come out of the walls of my study. I feel blessed to have known him.

———

THE BARD

$\mathcal{L}$ike most young men, the furthest thing from my mind when I attended high school were the perplexing plays of William Shakespeare. I well recall my first experience with the writings of the "Bard of Avon." It was my first year of high school, a month short of my fourteenth birthday. My English class was instructed to read *As You Like It*: I didn't! With all the "fare-you-wells," "hath nots," and especially ". . . I remember the kissing of her batlet and the cow's "dugs" that her pretty "chopt" hands had milked," I began to wonder what all the fuss was about; hell, when I was nine years of age, my grandfather decided that I didn't have enough to keep me occupied, and he, a devout Presbyterian, went to a local dairy, purchased a Guernsey cow, had it delivered to our home, and promptly informed me that the milk cow was my responsibility and that I was to milk her twice a day and, in general, take care of her. For the next year and a half, I milked that critter, stopping only the week following granddad's death. And though I had filled many a bucket with Daisy's white liquid, I had never squeezed a teat with a "pretty chopt" hand. Had I, I expect poor Daisy would have kicked over the milk bucket. Thanks to one particular professor, I began to understand and appreciate Shakespeare's works; the bard's coiffure I didn't!

Professor Robert Walsh, PhD., Fordham University, had one failing, especially if you happened to be sitting in the front row of his classroom: When he spoke, spittle would shower any poor varlet (Shakespearean word) within the good doctor's line of fire; it truly wreaked havoc on the bespectacled "rogue and peasant slave" (*Hamlet*, act 2, sc. 2).

Dr. Walsh, unlike many of his faculty colleagues, seldom consulted the written page when escorting our class through the acts and scenes of Shakespeare's plays; it seemed he had committed to memory the plays we studied under his tutelage. I recall one instance when, without benefit of a text, he awed us with his reading of Gloucester in *King Richard III*, his performance producing enough saliva to irrigate a small plant. Though we joked about his spitting, we deeply respected him; that is save for one other humorous eccentricity: his choice of neckwear.

He had, to our observation, but three four-in-hands, one sporting a hula dancer, one an oil derrick spewing a gusher, and another spotted with the giveaway signs of a few spaghetti dinners At semester's end, we presented him three ties, one a regimental stripe, a stylish and colorful paisley, and one with Bugs Bunny and Elmer Fudd emblazoned on a baby blue background; the old guy was overjoyed. However, he kept wearing the hula girl, oil derrick, and marinara patterned ties. We assumed that Bugs and Elmer were saved for weddings, funerals, and special occasions.

Though I never completely bought into Shakespeare, Dr. Walsh provided me a better understanding and appreciation for the Bard's works, a legacy I was able to pass on to my students when I became a teacher; through my association with him, I learned that when sporting a four-in-hand in an Italian restaurant, you requested always a large bib! Following my graduation, I kept in close touch with the good doctor until cancer took him in the late 1960s. My first thought upon learning of his passing concerned two lines from a poem by his favorite modern poet, Dylan Thomas:

"Do not go gentle into that good night. Rage, rage against the
dying of the light."

I'll wager he didn't and did!

USD has undergone change; it is much larger and not as warm. The sidewalk upon which Father Leo accosted me, demanding that I take on a role in his play is gone as is the classroom to which I was headed; the window that framed Father John's large head as he yelled to anyone within hearing distance remains still, and the room in which Dr. Walsh emoted Shakespeare to our amazed ears has become a part of the School of Law. But the shades of all three instructors stroll the school's halls seeking still the actor, the journalist, and the recalcitrant rascal bent on not learning to appreciate Shakespeare's elaborate wordplay; of course, there are two other men, living still to whom I must give thanks for their faith in me: Dean Parker is retired and living in Palm Springs, California; Fermin MacPhatter, in wheelchair still, lives in San Diego, California

(As noted in a previous sketch, these men have passéd away; this sketch was written earlier).

The debt I owe these men I can never repay; their names will forever be scrolled in the pantheon of my mind.

Graduation day came and went; ahead lay the first year of a thirty-eight year career as a high school instructor. It was during that initial year that I met yet another man who influenced me; it was under his tutorship that I was introduced to the rewards of teaching and the joys associated with pipe smoking.

HOME SWEET HOME

During my undergraduate days at USD, my wife and I were on a budget bordering on indigence. For want of more coin of the realm, we were forced to live in residences that, at times, resembled a monk's cell, they were so small. Our TV was a Magnavox, circa 1949, with a screen so small we were forced to sit at arm's length to see the Ed Sullivan Show; in addition, our antenna was a wire hanger thrown onto our apartment's roof, the TV's antenna wire loosely fastened to it. Our weekly night out usually consisted of a meal at an all-you-can-eat restaurant or an occasional inexpensive seafood dinner at a Chinese restaurant located on San Diego's Embarcadero, where the tight-pants waiter always served us extra French rolls. When the employees were not looking, Marion, as is her habit to this day, would stow the leftover bread in her oversize tote bag. The waiter's generosity? I think he may have had a crush on Marion (or me?).

I mentioned that we lived a small apartment. To better illustrate its smallness, allow me to carry you back in thought to New Year's Day, 1958. Having worked during school Christmas break at a local department store where I sold men's furnishing, I had picked up a little cash, and being a little flush for a change, Maid Marion and I decided to invite some good friends to the flat for dinner; we bought a ham, some sweet potatoes, the ingredients for a good salad, and, to top off the meal, a mincemeat pie and a quart of vanilla ice cream, the pièce de résistance—a bottle of cabernet sauvignon. That blew our budget for the next three weeks.

The guests invited, three couples we had known for years, the ham in the oven, its aroma permeating the apartment's every nook and cranny, we grappled with the problem of how to seat eight people in our close quarters. We agonized over the problem, but after a few days of shifting and moving, we arrived at the only solution possible.

The Rose Bowl game ended (OSU 10—Oregon 7). We seated our guests, two couples at one end of the table, two couples at the other end, one end projecting into the kitchen, the other end into the living room, a placing not inviting much conversation, but plenty of laughter. The ensuing years, as our income improved, our digs became more accommodating with enough floor space to seat twenty-eight to thirty dinner guests. But as is my custom, I regale the diners with the story of our New Year's supper in 1958. It always gets a chuckle from the gathering.

FOURTH AND SHORT

Introduction: In football's patois, the term "fourth and short" refers to a perplexing situation faced often by coaches: to play it safe and punt, or, if the coach is of the ilk of the late SC coach, John McKay, go for the first down with perhaps a little razzle-dazzle, a deceptive play, aimed at fooling the opponent's defense. Early in my marriage, faced with a "fourth and short" decision, I punted! But allow me to explain:

Entering the small apartment we had rented in East San Diego, I immediately sensed something was amiss; I could hear Marion, my wife of a few weeks, rattling some pots and pans in the kitchen. "I'm home, sweetie pie," I crooned, directing my honey-basted words toward the kitchen, which was actually a part of a living room that segued into our bedroom. The apartment was far too small to be defined as small; my little sister's dollhouse was larger.

Over the clanging of metal on metal, my wife's distinctive Chicago-accented voice, like Shakespeare's "scolding winds," came wafting into the living room, "I understand you're trying out for the school's football team, are you?"

How in hell's name did she find out? I was faced with a conundrum: to deny or own up to the question. "Football hero, you have two choices: me or football," her emphasis on the "me." I found myself situated between a hard spot and a seat on the team's bench. Of course, I really had little choice; without her financial help, I could ill afford to attend school. After five minutes of intense soul-searching, I reached my decision: "me," rather her. And a college football career was intercepted like an ill-thrown pass. My mistake had been my failure to apprise my bride of my desire to play the game. But I best begin at the beginning:

Close on the heels of my having been accepted as a member of the College for Men freshman class came a "call to arms" from the school's first football coach, Gil Kuhn, a member of the USC Trojan teams of the midthirties and captain of the 1935 squad. Kuhn and some well-meaning backers had convinced Bishop Charles F. Buddy, San Diego' Catholic prelate and founder of the University of San Diego, that fielding a collegiate football team could make USD the Notre Dame of the West, an idea that appealed to the bishop; however, what had not been explained to him was the expense involved in fielding a team. Furthermore, the bishop knew not the difference between a football and a pinball!

But I did, and since I had taken in my first football game in 1931 in the company of my aunt Mary Alice, a senior at Sweetwater High School. I had just recently turned five, but from the first kickoff, in a game pitting the Sweetwater Red Devils against the Grossmont High School Foothillers, I was hooked. But as much as I loved the game, I was never very good in its execution; in fact, in my formative years (six to ten, when teams were chosen in my neighborhood, my little sister, Gloria, was always chosen before I; perhaps the only reason I was ever asked to play was because I was the kid with the real football, one my aunt Mary Alice bought me every birthday until I was eleven. My little sis, on the other hand, was chosen over me not because she supplied the gang with a football but simply because she was more athletic than her brother. Two years younger than I was, she could punt, pass, and run the ass off about any boy on our block. And tough! On occasions when I got my tail whipped and ran home bawling, she often would step in and kick shit out of the guy who had kicked my ass. She was a wonderful athlete, and I hated her!

It wasn't until I was in junior high school that athletically I came into my own; by then, Sis had given up playing football, climbing trees, and beating shit out of half the neighborhood's boys. She even began wearing dresses, casting aside her previous raiment of jeans, tennis shoes, and sweatshirts. I, on the other hand, following a summer of working in the vegetable fields in the Tijuana Valley, had added two inches of height, put on a few pounds, and more importantly muscled up. Although I got screwed out of a football monogram, I earned letters in softball and track and field. I was ready for ninth-grade high school football at Madera Union High School located in California's San Joaquin Valley, where my sister and I were being unloaded on an Aunt and Uncle, the result of my grandmother breaking a hip and being hospitalized for God knows how long.

Happy about the prospect of living with relatives? Nope! Happy about the prospects of playing real football-yep-helmets, shoulder pads, jerseys with numbers front and back, shoes with cleats. In today's parlance, I was stoked, no more flag football as played at Southwest Junior High! Tackle! In a previous chapter, I discussed my introduction to high school ball, so I see little need in rehashing my experience other than to say that I lettered.

From that fall of 1941, my football playing was sporadic at best; in fact, the responsibility as "man of the house," thrust upon me by my grandmother's debilitating injury all but ended my budding gridiron career. Once I returned to San Diego, I was quickly locked into a war plant job that made no allowance for my dreams of becoming a swivel-hipped halfback; each afternoon found me in the employee of Solar Aircraft, shaping manifolds for B-24 bombers; while my more fortunate buddies scrimmaged after school under the coaching of Sweetwater's head coach, Gordon Cox, I was beating hell out of airplane parts. The money I earned helped in keeping the wolf away from the door of our small frame house in East San Diego.

Was it any wonder that at age twenty-eight, obsessed still by thoughts of gridiron glory, I threw in my lot, and a very out-of-shape body, with USD's first football team? But my dreams were shattered by a too logical wife: "You'll get killed! You're not a kid anymore," and the real assault on my ego, "You probably won't make the team anyway." But then came the unkindest cut of all, "You could be a cheerleader. You have a wonderful voice."

The suggestion cut me to the quick, the thought of my jumping around flailing my arms and yelling through a megaphone, urging the fans to "Lean to the left, lean to the right, stand up sit down, fight, fight, fight!" offended me, but upon reflection, I deduced that cheerleading would afford me a great spot from which to watch the game; I would be provided a snazzy sweater, and I would for the most part be center stage, a position I rarely enjoyed. So as the saying goes, the rest is history. Oh, I should mention that some of my cheers were so lascivious that I was summarily brought before the school's provost who informed me that we were a Catholic university and that my "bawdy cheers" would not be tolerated; Thus ended my football career and my one season as a "Yell-King."

Flash Forward: 2006.

Homecoming at the University of San Diego—besides the class reunion get-togethers, the 1956 football team would be recognized at the afternoon's football game, names enshrined in the pantheon of USD football. I, though not a member of that team, was awarded an honorary monogram and jacket (Perhaps because I bankrolled special commemorative caps for the extant members of the original squad). When I wear the jacket in public, I do with great frequency and pride. I am on the receiving end of strange looks, not to mention unflattering remarks such as "Jeez, dude, That old fart must be at least sixty. What the hell's he wearing a letterman's jacket for?"

"Well, for one thing, dud, you should not end a sentence with a preposition. Second, I am eighty, and you pimply-faced cretin, I reckon I can kick your ass as well as your lard-assed friend's."

Now, reader, do you grasp my reasons for abandoning a very successful teaching career?

V

Sixties and Seventies

GEORGE GROSS

$\mathscr{I}$t was the fall of 1960. Lacking a state of California teaching credential, I could not instruct in a public high school classroom; the only employment I was able to obtain that bordered on teaching was as a teacher's aide in the Grossmont Union High School District, specifically at Grossmont High school as a study hall monitor. My job was riding herd on 175 "students" in five "study" halls (Please note the quotes), the halls resembling the seventh and eighth circles of hell in Dante's *Divine Comedy*. Many of the youngsters were liars, cheats, blasphemers, thieves, and the like; some few were actually students, who used the fifty-five minutes of study hall to actually study. Although a pain in the ass to my teachers compared to these little shits, I had been a model student. The kids paid little heed to PA announcements and less attention to me. "You're not a real teacher. You're a flunky!" And so it went into early October, each day worse than the previous, and even though I had "been around the block," I was experiencing qualms about having taken the position at $2.75 an hour. Then one bright fall morning, a little bastard began working on my nerve endings.

His name was Bob, a pimple-faced runt, who made my first period mornings an absolute hell! Well, one morning push came to shove, and the excrement hit the fan! The second bell had rung at which time all students were to have their keisters ensconced in their desks; however, Master Bob was busy kibitzing with some of his lady friends.

"Excuse me, Bob, but would you and the young ladies please take your seats?"

There was no response to my request. I could feel my blood pressure rising as I again requested the youngsters to seat themselves. Stepping down from my desk platform, I approached Bob and his bevy of beauties. "Bob," I asked, "did you hear what I said?"

Glancing at each of the girls, as if preparing them for another of his stock-in-trade quips, he responded, a shit-eating grin on his face, "You can't tell me what to do, you son of a bitch." The punch I threw came off the floor, hitting the wiseass so hard that it knocked him over a row of desks into the next aisle. Quickly jumping to his feet, he demanded a pass to the principal's office. I just as quickly complied with his request; half hour later, I received a note from Mr. Barnett, the school's principal, directing me to report to his office during my prep period. I complied and was informed that the next day, a hearing had been scheduled between Bob's parents, Mr. Barnett, and me. Mr. Barnett assured me that though he didn't approve of my methods in dealing with the problem, he was "on my side." He proved a man of his word, defending me for about a minute before siding with the parents.

In the words of the father and mother, they would see to it that not only was I fired but also that I would never again serve in any capacity at Grossmont High School; Barnett, leaning back in his swivel chair, nodded his agreement. I just knew that I was going to be canned, but what I didn't realize was that help lay in the last three desks of Room 15: three varsity footballers who liked me.

Scheduled for termination during Thanksgiving weekend, I was dismayed, my dream of becoming a teacher seemingly remote, and with no jobs to be had, I began breaking out the work boots, flannel shirts, and Levis, convinced that soon I would be back behind the wheel of a lumber truck at Smith and Trevor Lumber Company; then, I received a phone call from the boy's father, who related how his son, in recounting the circumstances of the tiff, had failed to tell him about the name-calling, and although he and his wife were unwilling to forgive me my action, they, nonetheless, were withdrawing their complaint and requesting I be retained as the study hall monitor. However, they wanted their boy out of my study hall, a motion happily satisfying all parties.

But what had prompted this change of heart when a few days before, he, his spouse, and the gutless administrator, in their quest for my head, were upstaging the bloodthirsty Madame Defarge. The answer came a few months later.

A short time after the episode, a man sporting a crew cut entered my study hall and asked if my name was John Bowman. My first thought was that I was once again in trouble. But I had done nothing warranting another visit to the principal. "Yes," I sheepishly replied. "Why do you ask?"

He stated that he was department chairman of the school's English department, and he had it on good authority that I was an English major at USD and that my name had been mentioned to him by a USD faculty member with whom he had been a classmate at SDSU, following the end of World War II.

Business-like, he asked if I would consider becoming his aide, a position entailing the grading of papers, the tutoring of students placed under my supervision, and, in general, assisting in the running of his three senior English classes. He also stated that I would have the opportunity of lecturing a few classes on subject matter of my choosing.

"I have examined your transcripts and find that you are very strong in lit and composition." "Sir," I asked, "are you aware that I have been reprimanded by Mr. Barnett for striking a student?" He stated that he had been apprised of the problem, stated it had nothing to do with his offering me the position.

"So, how about joining me?" "Oh, by the way," he said, extending his right hand. "I'm George Gross."

As we shook hands, my eyes were riveted on the room's forty desks, occupied each school day by antsy youngsters. I accepted!

"Great," he rejoined. "I am looking forward to working with you. I'll see you in my office on Monday."

As he exited the room, the tagline of the 1950s TV comedian, George Goebel, caromed like a cue ball off the walls of my brain box: "real George."

Monday morning I entered Gross's "office," a large room, two or three tables positioned around the room, each table stacked high with textbooks; papers strewn all over and about the room, on chairs, on file cabinets, and seemingly in the room's every nook. Seated at a large oak desk, pipe in mouth, glasses on the end of his nose, I spotted Gross, pecking away on a typewriter. The room reeked of a redolent English brand of pipe tobacco, rich and pungent, conjuring thoughts of my days spent shooting snooker in Bob Ryan's billiard parlor.

"Come in, John. Make yourself at home." Shoving aside his Underwood, Gross put a match to the bowl of his straight-stemmed Canadian briar.

"You smoke, John?"

"Yes," I sheepishly responded. "Two packs of Camels a day."

"I'll have to get you off those coffin nails and get you started smoking a good briar."

I had tried smoking a pipe while in the service, finding it a pain in the ass, hauling the paraphernalia: pipe cleaners, tamper, kitchen matches, and tobacco pouch. Besides, my clothes ended up full of holes caused by errant hot ashes. Nope, I thought, I will stick with my easily transported packs. Umph! No briars for me.

Two weeks later found me contentedly puffing away on a pipe purported to be crooner Bing Crosby's briar of choice. Afternoons found Gross and me filling the office workroom with a blue, aromatic fog, prompting pleas for air from students engaged in tutorial sessions. Me? I thought the pipe gave me a more professorial look; my spouse, in a snit, thought the pipe smoke was reeky; whatever, I had puffed my last Camel.

What with running herd on the students in two study halls, tutoring in Gross's junior and senior English classes, and occasionally, with Gross's permission, lecturing a few times, the year quickly drew to a close. Between puffs on our pipes and sips of our acid-inducing coffee, Gross and I talked, and the more we talked, the more I learned about the proper approach to teaching the adolescent; he proved not only an excellent teacher but also more importantly a good and respected friend.

In late spring, he accepted a teaching position at San Diego State University; I, on the other hand, was about to join the ranks of the unemployed. On the verge of telephoning my old boss at the lumber yard, I received a call from a friend informing me that Saint Augustine High School in San Diego was looking for a teacher of English, no standard teaching credential needed. I applied. Carrying a letter of reference from George and an unofficial transcript from USD, I was hired to teach. My salary was $4,000 per annum; however, after making a whopping $2.75 an hour at the high school, $400 a month was a step-up. I signed a contract for the 1961-62 term. I was to teach freshman English and senior Civics, as well as assist coaching track and field. That first year set the stage for a run of seventeen years and the beginning of thirty-six productive and rewarding years in the classroom.

A few days later at semester's end, the other three aides and I treated George to lunch. During the table conversation, the truth about the fabled student slugging came to light from the mouth of my mentor. I had always assumed the boy of his own volition had come forward, admitting to his parents that he had lied about the facts leading to the incident. Between sips of his coffee, George announced to us that my position as aide had been through the efforts of the three football players in my study hall, who, upon learning of the possibility of my being fired, threatened to kick shit out of Bob if he didn't come clean to his mother and father.

My relationship with George Gross did not end that spring of 1961. Over the course of ensuing years, I availed myself of George's largesse in assisting me in the solving of curriculum problems; he always had time for conferences at his home, visits that produced not only solutions to my needs but also a bracing cup of coffee, his wife's home-baked cookies, and, of course, a couple of bowls filled with our favorite tobacco, all adding up to a "real George" afternoon.

PS: To this day, I am a pipe smoker and coffee hound, and I have stained teeth to prove it.

THE VOICE OF THE
SAN DIEGO PADRES

$\mathcal{T}$o those individuals too young to remember, the San Diego "Padres" in the 1960s, a member of the Pacific Coast League, played their games in Westgate Park, a cozy little ballpark situated where today's Westfield shopping center is located; in fact, home plate was but a few feet from what is now the east entrance to Bloomingdale's. Small, seating just a shade over five thousand fans, Westgate was the antithesis of today's cavernous, indifferent, and high-priced ballparks, heartless concrete and steel arenas, caring little for the fans frequenting them, seemingly interested only in how much money they can squeeze from them, making it well nigh impossible for a family of four to take in more than a few games during the season. Conversely, Westgate Park was small; compared to today's construction costs, built for a pittance, but more importantly caring for its fans' comfort and their financial solvency; furthermore, its management team was headed by Eddie Leishmann, a much respected baseball man of many years experience and the reason for my part-time career as the voice of the San Diego.

It was the spring of 1961. As stated in the previous chapter, I had been hired as a teacher's aide/study hall proctor at a local public high school; however, my $2.75 per hour was adding little mazuma to the family's coffer; fortunately, through a stroke of luck, our income increased when I became the public address announcer for the PCL Padres.

Blessed with a resonant voice and the gift of articulation, or as my spouse put it "endowed with a big mouth," in the fall of 1960, Bob King, the University of San Diego's Sport's Information director, asked me to take over the public address announcing for the school's football team's home games. Without hesitation, I accepted the job at $5 per game, the five-game gig promising the addition of an extra $25 to my weekly pay of $66.50 at the high school. My work on the football games proved the catalyst in my transition from the voice of the University of San Diego "Pioneers" to the voice of the San Diego "Padres." My break into professional baseball as a PA announcer came on an evening in April 1961 as I sauntered into Westgate Park to take in the collegiate baseball game between the University of Notre Dame and the University of San Diego.

I had just picked up a program and a bag of popcorn when I heard the distinctive vocal intonations of Hawaiian-born Bob King, "How about doing this game for us, Johnny?"

My first thought was to thank him but refuse his request; however, knowing that I would enjoy the game more from high in the press box, I accepted, and, thanking Bob, made my way up the catwalk to the public address announcer's booth. What had begun as a favor to a good friend led to a ten-year part-time job for which many dyed-in-the-wool baseball buffs would have mortgaged their homes. But back to the "Irish" and "Pioneers" game.

The game was a blowout for the lads from South Bend; in other words, it was boring. Hot dogs and beer were distributed throughout the press box, providing the highlights through the sixth inning. Then, with two outs in the "Irish" top of the seventh, I sensed someone standing behind me.

After the inning's final out, I made an announcement concerning USD's sponsors; swiveling my chair around, my eyes came in contact with two people, one a spare-bodied, elderly gentleman, the other, a handsome, strapping teen.

"Don't let us bother you, son," said the gentleman. "You've a great voice, and you're doing splendidly," he added.

The kid just stood, statue like, a shit-eating grin on his face. Thanking the man, I turned back to the mic for another commercial announcement and a change in pitchers for the USD nine, the reliever faring no better than had the team's starters. I was focused on the exodus from the stands, when a long-fingered hand placed something into the breast pocket of my corduroy sport jacket. "Nice job, young man. Give me a call next Monday." My eyes riveted on the field of play, I raised my right arm and tendered my thanks. I heard the announcing booth door's distinguishable metallic click, and they were gone. Bottom of the ninth; Westgate Park's seating area was, save for one diehard fan, empty. "Leading off for the 'Pioneers,' Terry Lorenz, third base." A couple of outs later, I packed up and went home, two bags of peanuts in my jacket pockets. (My wife loved goobers.)

Emptying my pockets on the dresser, I pulled a card from the left breast pocket of my sport's jacket. It read, "Edward Leishmann, General Manager, San Diego Baseball Club." Then, remembering his having asked me to phone him on Monday, I spent perhaps the longest weekend I had ever experienced, mentally fielding what he might possibly throw at me: stock in the ball club, sports information officer, concessions' manager, groundskeeper, hot dog hawker, or, heaven forbid, batboy? At seven o'clock Mass on Sunday, at the Prayer of the Faithful, I egotistically prayed for some sort of position with the ball club, tacking on an "Our Father and a Hail Mary," figuring I needed all the spiritual backing I could muster. Monday afternoon proved that some heavenly dignitary had heard my orisons.

On Monday, cutting short my tutoring schedule a shade after noon, I arrived home where I quickly dialed the ballpark's office. "Mr. Leishmann is out of the office right now. Could I have him call you?" Leaving my telephone number with the receptionist, I set about grading some essays that were to be returned on Wednesday. It was evident from the verbal bullshit attempting to be passed off as good composition that the school year was almost at an end and that summer vacation was on the horizon. As I plodded my way through a bog of misspelled words, illogical reasonings, incorrect word choices, and sentence fragments, the phone rang. Apprehensively I put the receiver to my ear.

"Am I speaking with John Bowman?" Recognizing the warm and mellow voice as that of Mr. Leishmann, my nervousness was quickly put to rest. Yes, it was. "John, How'd you like to take over public address duties at Westgate Park?" Without so much as asking what I would be paid, I accepted. "Can we expect you to start on our next home stand?" I replied in the affirmative. "We'll pay you $10 a game, $15 for doubleheaders. Does that sound fair?" I accepted unconditionally his offer. "Then, son, we'll see you at the ballpark on April 26 when we begin a five-game series with Portland." I assured him he would. "Glad to have you as part of our team. Good-bye for now."

It hadn't been five minutes since our conversation, and I was already figuring how much money I would make during the course of the season, presently in its third week. I figured I wouldn't amass a fortune, but the extra income would, like the income from my teacher's aide job, greatly contribute to our household budget. I was overjoyed at the prospects of putting my pipes to work, little realizing that in a few weeks, those prospects would include hearing from folks I hadn't had contact with in years: "Hey, John, could fix me up with a few freebies to the Denver game? Me? Fred Bickle, you know from fifth grade at San Ysidro Elementary." Hell, my only remembrance of Fred was that he used to kick shit out of me with great regularity. One guy, with whom I had at one time sat across from in USD's cafeteria, phoned, requesting sixteen tickets; it seemed he had relatives from Ohio visiting, and he wanted to impress them. And so it went for ten years in the announcer's booth, hundreds of requests for free ticket from folks I barely remembered. But the job had its bright side.

I wasn't into the gig for more than two years when I began getting offers of other PA jobs throughout the San Diego area: San Diego State University hired me as its PA man for "Aztec" football and basketball. USD retained me as its "man at the mic" for football and basketball. I was even considered for the PA job with the San Diego "Chargers" NFL team, losing out to a local disc jockey who sported a brown nose. I even filled in once at a San Diego "Clippers" game, San Diego's first NBA team (Remember Elvin Hayes?); however, though pleased with the extra jobs and local recognition, I was most pleased with an article written in a Tijuana newspaper which loosely translated stated that I was the only American public address announcer who knew the first thing about the pronunciation of Hispanic surnames. My Spanish-born grandmother, looking down from heaven, must have been sporting a Galician smile. But despite my success, my spouse continued insisting that I got the job because I "had a big mouth."

I eventually lost my position with the "Padres" to that disc jockey toady, and the phone calls from acquaintances from former times ceased. But rather than dwell on the tragic, I wish to leave you with an amusing incident that happened during my fifth season. I was hired by a boys' Catholic high school to teach English and Civics, a position I held for seventeen years. All the students knew that I was PA man for the Padres; they, too, were aware that I could get free passes to games, and, of course, they were constantly badgering me for tickets. Finally, having had my fill of the annoying requests, I informed my juniors that on a first-come-first-served basis, I would procure five tickets for local games. Of course, adolescents have, from the dawn of history, possessed a decided talent for making up their own rules, resulting in punitive measures. Just such an incident occurred in 1965.

The "Padres" were in the second game of a five-game home stand against the Portland "Beavers." The third inning over, I was about to relieve myself of the three colas I had imbibed, when there was a knock at my door. It was Bob Lanntz, the ballpark's head of security, who requested I follow him to the top of the catwalk that led to the press box. Standing there were two juniors from my American literature class, both grinning like jackasses who had just eaten thistles.

Almost apologetically, Bob announced that the lads had been caught hopping the fence to gain admittance. "They say they know you, that you are one of their teachers at St. Augustine High," Bob stated.

Casting a disdainful look at both kids, I remarked, "I've never before seen either of them."

Then I did an about-face and headed for the restroom, not sticking around to note the looks on their smug kissers. The next day the shit hit the fan. "How come you didn't stick up for us, JB?" I explained that I had clearly established a system whereby I would get tickets for them and that I was truly annoyed that they took it upon themselves to ignore my offer and attempt to gain admittance to the ballpark by jumping the fence, and, furthermore, I warned that the next time any one of them decided he would sneak into the park, I was going to see that he landed in the slammer for trespassing. They took me at my word and decided that requesting a couple of freebies beat hell out of spending time in jail.

Go Saints

*T*he spring of 1961 found me facing unemployment, the first-semester's altercation and subsequent punch to the nose of the imprudent student branding me an educational pariah. I was finished as an employee of the Grossmont School District. Once again, I faced the prospect of returning to the lumber yard or, worse, to flipping burgers in a fast-food eatery.

Although holding a bachelor of arts degree in English/literature, I possessed not a California Teacher's Credential, a piece of paper essential to landing a teaching position in the public schools. Fortunately, a couple of weeks into July, I received a telephone call from St. Augustine High School, an all-boys Catholic secondary school located in San Diego's North Park district. I had, following my problem at GHS, submitted, accompanied by my college transcripts, a letter informing the school that I would be available for hire in the fall; furthermore, I was a Roman Catholic in good standing, an altar boy in my youth, and a regular contributor to my parish's coffers; also included was a wonderful letter from George Gross, extolling my talents as an English teacher, a person perfectly suited to interesting young men in prose and poetry. George made no mention of my pugilistic gifts!

On a day in early July, I received a phone call from the school's receptionist. It seemed, I was informed, that the person who had been hired in the spring to teach freshman English and civics had opted to take a more lucrative job as a technical writer for a local aircraft company, and as I was the only remaining applicant, the school's principal wondered if I would be interested. Interested? You bet I am; when do I come in?

"Friday afternoon at two."

"I'll be there. Thank you."

Friday afternoon found me standing before a priest who resembled Samuel Johnson, the eighteenth century English lexicographer, essayist, poet, and moralist, once described by his biographer James Boswell as "a bear of a man."

"So, Mr. Bowman," growled the man-bear, "you think you would like to join our faculty?"

Neglecting to tell him that I was in need of a job, I played it cool, giving him a terse answer, "Yes, Father."

"Well," he stated, scanning a paper held in his grizzly bear-sized paw, "a perusal of these letters of recommendation indicate that you come to us highly commended. My close friend Father John Bremner feels you are gifted, a person able to fuse his diverse life experiences with the presentations of life as found in works of literature. That's a talent possessed by few teachers." I began feeling a tad better. "Now," continued the good father, his stentorian voice resounding out of his office, into the administrative office's halls, "how does $4,000 sound to you?"

"Father," I retorted. "Four thousand a month sounds very fair."

"No, Mr. Bowman, not a month, for the school year."

Gulp! Not a math whiz, I quickly deduced that I was looking at $100 a week, $20 a day, and the princely sum of $4 a class for a five classes. I was giving serious thought of returning to the lumberyard.

"Of course," continued the priest-principal, "you'll be expected to take on a few extracurricular activities in addition to your regular teaching assignment."

The pay? "Nothing extra," the padre answered, between puffs on an odoriferous cigar that looked about a foot long. "Here at Saint Augustine, we all share the load."

My first thought was that the Havana on which he was puffing probably cost what I would be making per diem. But, hell, what he offered exceeded what I was making, although not by much. "Where do I sign, Father?" My signing of that contract was a decision I never regretted; I will forever be beholden to my students, who have been my joy and my sometimes tender torment.

PS: Because the school had no retirement plan for its faculty, I was forced, in 1977, to look elsewhere for employment, locating one teaching position at Ramona Union High School located in San Diego County, where I successfully taught and coached for eighteen years, retiring in 1993 at age sixty-seven.

TIME OR NEWSWEEK

It was 1963. A few weeks before the school broke for Christmas vacation, my Civics classes were driving me crazy, which at an all-boys' school wasn't difficult. The first eleven weeks of the fall semester I had been teaching out of an antiquated textbook that might well have been authored by a gathering of Druids at Stonehenge, a book totally out of sync with the twentieth century. Then, as if a message from the spirit of John Dewey, United States philosopher and educator, an idea. I felt it would remove my fears of having to face another unnerving semester and, in the process, enlighten the minds of the class dolts. The answer: subscriptions to publications of a political bent, namely *Time* or *Newsweek*.

So, it came to pass, two weeks before breaking for the holidays, I announced that in their letters to Santa, the lads were to request subscription to one of the two weeklies; the choice I left to them. Oh, such a hue and cry filled the classrooms. One lad, unable to control his ire, shouted, "That's bullshit, Mr. Bowman!" Bullshit or no bullshit, I informed the classes that they were being held responsible for having in their grimy paws, on their return to class the second week of the new year, a copy of *Time* or *Newsweek*; failure to comply with my directive would result in some extreme disciplinary measures. I never idly threatened, and they all knew it and, oddly enough, respected me for it.

Christmas and New Years observed and celebrated, classes reconvened amid the mindless, inarticulate prattle of a horde of teenaged boys who made an art of misusing the phrases, "you know," and "it's like." As the lads filed into Room 13 that day, I looked for signs that my Christmas mandate had been followed, that each member of the class had a copy of one or the other weeklies. "OK! Let's get some quiet in this room. Vacation is over, and it's time to get back to work. As I take roll, stand, and hold up, at arm's length, your copy of *Newsweek* or *Time* so I can plainly see it. If I catch any of you attempting to pass your copy to another guy, I will make certain that your first day back in class will not be without repercussions." I began calling roll, the "lucid stillness"

(T. S. Eliot) broken only by my stentorian voice. Just one lad failed to produce a magazine, and he, unfortunately, was absent, confined at home attempting to fight a flu bug; however, in a telephone conversation with his mother later that afternoon, I learned he had subscribed to not one but both magazines. One smart-ass tried to convince me that I should accept *Sports Illustrated*; another wisenheimer suggested I was getting a kickback from Time-Life Publications. And from the back of the room came this muffled, featherbrained suggestion, "Playboy"? I was having difficulty suppressing an urge to laugh.

I suppose at this juncture you are asking yourself, "What in the hell does all this business about magazines have to do with this chapter?" Patience, good reader; I shall explain. This piece of fluff was spawned at the class of 1964s' fortieth reunion. In recalling memories of the class's four years at St. Augustine High School, the one memory that took precedence in our conversation was the semester when they were required weekly reading of either *Newsweek* or *Time*; in addition, they were tested weekly on the magazines' different sections: sports; national news, international news, entertainment, commerce, etc. In other words, during the course of the spring semester, each student was tested on some one section of the magazine he was expected to read, the only catch being that the students never knew which section and, therefore, they were forced to read the entire edition on that given week including the advertisements.

They thought they had it tough! I, too, was required to read not one but two magazines a week; in addition, I had to create two different tests, one for the readers of *Time* and one for those lads reading *Newsweek*. Of course, it was unfair. As one youngster so ably put it, "Mr. Bowman, you could have taught Torquemada a few things about torture." (At least, the kid had been paying attention when he had studied the Spanish Inquisition.) But as Master William Shakespeare put it so succinctly, "All's well that ends eell." Forty-plus years later, by their own admissions, more than half of the lads from those classes are still reading *Time* or *Newsweek*. And, no, I am not getting any kickback from either publishing house.

FATHERHOOD

"*He* that is childless has no light in his eyes."(Persian Proverb) "It's a girl!" I remember well that night, half asleep, seated on a too comfortable divan in the lobby of Heartland Hospital and being startled into a state of consciousness by the voice of Dr. Herman Rauch.

This afternoon, seated at this word processor, myriad thoughts of that evening flood my mind: My wife's lengthy lying-in in the wee hours of February 15, our scurrying around the house gathering sundry items such as her cosmetic bag, her bed jacket, and her insurance cards. Then, I remember, clothed only in my drawers and bathrobe, speeding through the darkened streets of Spring Valley and El Cajon, half expecting, as I had seen in numerous movies, a motorcycle policeman pulling along side my MG and, upon discovering that the sports car's passenger was in-a-family way, signaling me to follow him, his pulsating red lights, his siren's shrill wail knifing through the early morning mist. I spotted not one cop in our ten-mile sprint to the hospital. The birthing of our first child was no romp in the park for my wife, who spent almost eighteen hours in labor before delivering us a beautiful baby girl whom we named Bernadette Frances; she, and her three siblings, born over the next four years, were to change my life forever.

Frances, named for her great-aunt, was a precocious child, reading before she was four, curious, articulate, and bright for her years; never a day passed without her doing something that I unloaded on an unsuspecting faculty the following day at lunch in the school's lounge.

One such event happened shortly after Thanksgiving in 1967; Francis was five. One evening as I was reclining in the folds of my favorite chair, reading the daily sports page in the *San Diego Tribune*, Francie, seated on the floor at my feet, thumbing through a copy of my latest National Geographic, asked me what a "duck-billed plateepus" was. In a typical distracted father form, I replied, my eyes and mind never taking leave of the sports page, "Sweetheart, the duck-billed platypus is an egg-laying mammal."

"Daddy," responded my towhead. "I want Santa to bring me one for Christmas." I absentmindedly answered, "OK, doll, I'll write a letter to Santa the first chance I get." Case closed? Nope!

Christmas morning, in typical California Yuletide weather, dawned sunny and warm, our living room floor stacked high with gifts of every ilk, our best laid plans to keep the holiday simple and within our budget shot to hell, one half of the living room floor an island of beautifully wrapped packages that soon would be ripped to shreds, wrapping paper, and ribbons strewn the length and width of the room.

Everything seemed normal: Three-year-old Molly cuddled her new dolly; the twins, Eileen and Conway, aged one crawled around the floor, both paying little heed to direction, both threatening to topple the Christmas tree, while, seated in a nest of holiday wrappings, Frances cried like a Minnesota lake loon. "Jesus, Mary, and Joseph, what's the matter with that child?" I demanded of my wife, who, ensconced upon the couch, was busily trying on the sporty cashmere sweater I had purchased for her at Lion's Clothiers (only the best for the little woman). "Well, dear, why don't you ask her?" Wading my way through a tidal pool of ribbon and multicolored papers, I cautiously approached the child, her copious tears streaming down her cherubic cheeks. "Why are you crying, sweetheart?" I questioned in felicitous fatherly fashion. "You have a lovely dollhouse that Daddy spent half the night putting together; a chatty Cathy doll; a china tea set Grandma Conway brought you from Chicago, the set of children's classics Aunt Frances and Uncle Paul bought for you in Cincinnati. Don't forget the stable of beautiful horses Santa left under the tree. Aren't you happy with these gifts?" There was silence.

"What is the matter, dear?" I questioned.

Between sobs, she blurted, "Santa is sumabisch!" (No plateepus!)

A shocked and disgusted Grandma McVeigh, in a frenzy, was quick to point her arthritically gnarled finger at me, declaring that I was responsible for the child's crudity, "Didn't I warn you, Marion, that one day you would be sorry allowing him to spew that filthy talk around these children?"

My wife, absorbed in nibbling at a slice of Christmas "kuchen," merely nodded and replied, "Yes, Mom, you did."

Aunt Frances, a teen flapper during the Roaring Twenties, merely smiled, apparently tickled at Frannie's cultivated vocabulary; Uncle Paul, oblivious to the living room drama happening around him, sat in my Lazy Boy chair, puffing contentedly on his Missouri meerschaum. Me? I was surprised my mother-in-law hadn't hied herself to church to light a few votive candles for the souls of Frances and her old man. This episode in my life's story ends on a happy note; two notes to be precise.

Frannie had been attending Catholic preschool since September, and upon her return following Christmas vacation, she and her little classmates were seated in a semicircle singing "Old MacDonald had a Farm" and requested by their teacher to supply the name of an animal after each verse (". . . and on his farm he had a _____") The class of tykes would fill in the blank by yelling loudly and gleefully. During a parents' and teachers' night some weeks later, Frannie's teacher, Mrs. Corte, recounted that on that particular day, as the class was singing the song and it came time to sing out an animal, a very tiny voice piped in with, ". . . and on his farm he had a duck-billed plateepus." Mrs. Corte said she wheeled around in her swiveled chair, anxious to find out which child had chimed in with the remark, and in the back row she saw Frannie, a beautiful smile on her face. Needless to say, the teacher was amazed that a child of such tender years would have heard of the Australian mammal, much less been able to pronounce its name; of course, I wasn't surprised. She took after her old man.

Some years later, as Frannie approached her thirty-ninth year, I was at the end of my rope, trying to figure what I could buy her; I was stumped until I happened to walk into a toy store, and there on a shelf of toy animals was, of all things, a duck-billed platypus! At her birthday party, I presented her the stuffed animal accompanied by this declarative sentence, "That sumabisch Santa finally came through!" Grandma McVeigh probably turned over in her grave!

The four children, now in their forties, continue making me proud but more importantly remain a constant reminder of how lucky I am to be their father. All have experienced different career callings, Frances, who now answers to Bernadette, is a producer of DVD special features; Molly, married to a TV meteorologist, parlayed her undergraduate and graduate degrees from the University of San Diego into a career in Public Affairs; the twins, Conway and Eileen, are successful, each in his own way, Conway a rising star in Outdoor Life television; Eileen, also married, a member of the Screen Actors' Guild, keeps busy doing local theater and television commercials.

Proud of them? You bet I am; more importantly, each youngster is proud of what he has made of his life. Dad? Aside from my pride in their individual accomplishments, I view each of them as my conscience, and before I even consider doing something out of the ordinary, I ask myself this question, "How will my action affect the children?" My love for them is unconditional, and I consider a blessing the day each was born. They turned my life around and, as the Persian philosopher said, "put a light in my eyes."

GIN AND DRY VERMOUTH
DON'T CATCH FISH

*T*he lad sat dejectedly on the front edge of my office couch, hand kneading hand, eyes glued to the floor, while I intentionally ignored him by aimlessly shuffling through a stack of detention referrals. Finally, convinced that I had made him sweat enough, and peering over the tops of my glasses, I requested he stop fidgeting and sit up straight. He did. Why had I, on Mass day, caught him smoking pot in the alley behind the school? Parrying my question, he skillfully reversed our roles, I the defendant, he the prosecutor.

"I suppose, sir, that when life becomes a pain in the ass you hit a local bar and throw back a few martinis!"

I assured him that my imbibing had nothing to do with life's pressures, but, yes, I enjoyed a martini on occasion; however I admitted I much better enjoyed a dram of good, single malt scotch whiskey.

The shit-eating "I gotcha grin" on the kid's mug sent a message: He thought he had me by the "family jewels." He was, however, mistaken; I unloaded a curveball, low and away.

"Scott, when I find myself under pressure, whatever the source, I pick up my fly rod, chest waders, and a few wet and dry flies and go fishing."

Suddenly the smugness was erased like a grammatical error on a blackboard. The young man sat, chopfallen as Master Shakespeare would say; he left my room, scratching his head and muttering, "He goes fishing!?"

So I suppose you're asking, "What the hell does all this have to do with this chapter?"

Well, ask no more; I am about to enlighten you.

For years I had dabbled in the sport of fishing: as a lad with cane pole and worm in the ponds formed by the Tijuana River; later, as a teenager I was accompanied by my uncle on half-day boats in the kelp beds off the San Diego coast. However, it was not until my junior year in college that I truly began to think of the pastime as more than a means of escaping the boredom of weekend yard work, for it was that year that I worked at a war surplus store in downtown San Diego for a man named Jim Martinez, manager of the store's sporting goods department. We sold camping equipment, tents, cookware, pots, pans, coffeepots, canteens, and all the other paraphernalia one associates with roughing it in the wilds. In addition, our department included a well-stocked fishing section: rods, reels, line, hooks, as well as the latest artificial lures guaranteed to "hook" the prospective angler. But the gear that really caught my eye was in the fly-fishing section, a division of angling with which I had little or no knowledge, assuming it was limited to either the very rich or to the Olympian gods.

But introduction to the Brotherhood of the Jungle Cock was close at hand in the person of my boss, Jim Martinez, a transplanted New Mexican, born in the shadows of the Sangre de Cristo Mountains, an area of small trout streams and high mountain lakes, a veritable fly-caster's paradise, where the waters teem with rainbow and brown trout. It was he who introduced me to the joys and wonders of casting the fly to surface-dimpling "trucha." I was hooked!

In the months that followed, having stowed my spinning reels and rods away in my tackle locker, I began fly-fishing, first employing a cheap Japanese fly rod, the type bought by military men stationed in Japan; then, as my casting improved, I graduated to a graphite rod. I was soon deserting the local lakes and their schools of sunfish for the trout streams of Oregon, Idaho, Arizona, and Montana. My education in the art of fly-fishing became progressive, each year advancing me into another facet of the sport, but, perhaps, what I truly gleaned from my immersion into the world of fly-fishing was a means to an end during my thirty-eight years spent as a high school teacher.

Early in my career, I quickly realized that many students not involved in athletics or other school extracurricular activities often felt excluded from the day-to-day campus pursuits. I, therefore, set about the task of organizing an angling club, hoping to attract those lonesome souls who, afternoon after afternoon, forlornly wandered the campus grounds, unhappy kids with little to do during their downtime, kids lacking that one thing that would fill the void in their lives.

The day I announced that I was forming a fishing club, dozens of youngsters formed a queue outside my classroom door; by school day's end, I had enlisted thirty-five prospective Izaak Waltons; thus, the St. Augustine High School's Angling Society was born, and for the next six years proved one of the most rewarding and active clubs on campus. Furthermore, it was more than just a means of getting your picture in the yearbook. There were rules governing a student's participation: All members were required to maintain at least a C-plus grade average, were expected to receive passing grades in citizenship, and were expected to obey the club's bylaws.

In 1977, I left the Catholic school for the greener (as in money) pastures of the public school system, the club meeting its demise fewer than three months after my departure, perhaps because it was always rumored that "Bowman founded the club for his own benefit." Nothing could have been further from the truth; my reasons were selfish in that I wanted the young men to take from fishing what I did: On a lake or trout stream amid nature's (God's) handiwork, we quickly conclude that we are not the most important atom in the universe. In the words of former President Herbert Hoover, himself a very passable fly angler, "All men are equal in the eyes of a trout."

So you continue to ask, "What in the hell has all this to do with a kid caught smoking pot?"

It means that there are many avenues available to kids who are troubled, fishing is but one; however, fishing offers more than catching and releasing a creature with a pin-sized brainpan. It also teaches respect, responsibility, and accountability. In the six years I was the club's moderator, I can recall only one instance of a kid's impropriety: He was caught with too many fish on his stringer, a breach of our club's bylaws.

Scott, the kid who thought I was nuts? I heard recently on the alumni grapevine that he's the CEO for a large clothing chain. I don't know if he ever took up fishing, but he might be happy to know that I, on occasion, throw back a dram of good, single malt scotch.

LINEMEN SPARE THAT
TWEED SPORTS COAT!

$\mathcal{G}$ranted, I wasn't the best football coach in San Diego, but I was ever the best-dressed. Like my hero, Tom Landry of the Dallas Cowboys, I sported the tweed jacket, knit tie, button-down-oxford-cloth dress shirt, well-creased grey flannel slacks, and black wing-tipped brogans. As a coach, my skills lay in my ability to ass-kick and to make even the ancient Greeks forget Stentor, that loudmouthed herald of the Trojan Wars, and although I could intimidate, I found X's and O's merely letters in the alphabet. I believe my tenure as a football coach was the result of the Catholic Boys' School's need for a coach who would work cheaply; they found a willing, underpaid, candidate in me.

1965: Bill Whittaker, a legend among San Diego's coaching fraternity, had been a coach since Alonzo Stagg had coached the University of Chicago, or so it seemed. Somewhere in the school's monastery, a decision was made to pair Bill and me as coaches of the Saint Augustine junior varsity football team. [As an English/literature teacher I had made my mark, but the only coaching I had ever done was training my three-year-old daughter to eat her Cream of Wheat! Football?

Sure I loved football, a game I had learned to love from the age of six, after my grandfather had taken me to a University of Southern California game in Los Angeles in 1932. True I had played a little in high school and had gone out for the football team at USD, but coach!? Father Principal had to be out of his anointed mind! I could explain to young men Hemingway's use of the understatement, or Steinbeck's works' allusions to Mallory's Arthurian legends, or the vulgarity found in Chaucer's "Canterbury Tales," but, hell, the only "passing lane" I knew was on a highway. It was the money, not much, but a little more money to fill our bare-coffers, so I joined forces with Big Bill, and

---

218

together we managed, through Bill's knowledge of the game, and my constant badgering, to develop a respectable, though losing, eleven.

The team, made up of mostly sophomores, though talented, was really inexperienced, their record toward season's conclusion showing more "L's" than "W's," a statistic clearly reflecting that the coaching also lacked experience, especially that of the line coach (guess who?). Our final game of the season was against one of our in-city rivals—the Crawford High School "Colts," the league's leaders when we met them of their field on an overcast Friday afternoon in November.

After a prep talk by Big Bill, the team emptied the bus and headed for the field, a gridiron that smelled like the Chicago stock yards. "Geez!," one of our gridiron grenadier's exclaimed, "the damned field is as spongy as a swamp and covered in horse shit!" Horse shit?! Big Bill and I conned the manure blanketing the field, large horse turds decorating the field from end-zone to end-zone. Bill, never one to miss an opportunity to fire up a team, blurted, "Men, they think you aren't worth a shit!" All hell broke loss; the kids were huffing and puffing like fighting bulls at a Mexican corrida. The lads were ready to kick some ass, and they did, defeating the favored "Colts" by two points, priming them for shoulder-carrying some adult asses off the field—their coaches.

Their jerseys and pants covered in fetid smears of horse crap, they made for Bill, determined to carry him from the field of battle like a triumphant Roman gladiator. Now, this is where the story gets interesting. Just a week before the game, I had purchased a neat, grey, tweed jacket for thirty-eight bucks, a princely sum for the father of two infant daughters and a guy making but $6,500 a year. God was I proud of that sport coat. I had dressed-to-the-nines for the game, new jacket, white shirt, black knit tie, dark-grey flannels and black-and-white saddle shoes (Hey, Mr. B,. are you going bowling?). Smart asses!! Anyway, I looked sharp.

Turning to congratulate the team, I spied Bill, attired as usual in sweat pants, Saints' jacket and a ball cap that had seen better days, atop the shoulders of two of the sweaty, smelly, feces-coated linebackers, swarms of buzzing flies and shouting players milling around them. Then, out of the corner of my beady eyes, I noticed half-dozen good-sized linemen slinking toward me, their crazed eyes zeroed in on me and my new jacket. Heeding my instincts, I took off like a shot, the six galoots in pursuit, all yelling, "Let's get him!" As I fled, a thought kept running through my mind, "They're going to smear horse droppings on my sport coat!" I made a run to El Cajon Boulevard where I caught a bus to my home in La Mesa.

The next Monday at school Bill asked, "Why didn't you wear old clothes to the game, John?" What, and ruin my image? No, sir, as long as I coach, I will dress like Tom Landry, Vince Lombardi, and Paul "Bear" Bryant, sans hat, of course, and horse crap be damned!

THE PERFECT LEAD

$\mathscr{I}$t was the spring of 1967. I was pissed! My junior American literature class was giving me fits. Four weeks till the end of the term and their compositions were shit! Thirty-one guys in the class, and not one had submitted a decent paper; those submitted were better suited to the bottom of a birdcage or ass-wipe in a farmyard privy. How could I get the laggards to turn in some passable work, a lead sentence that gave promise of a good read, a paper so damned good that it challenged me to find error in its makeup? But the real problem lay in the lads' failure to create a good lead sentence, a clause promising to knock off my socks, an idea demanding to be read, brainwork demanding logical development.

But was I receiving papers of this ilk? Hell, no! What I received and had been receiving for the past six weeks were reams of verbal pabulum! I decided to take a stand in the matter, to challenge, nay threaten, the dolts with failing grades were not my demands met; so it came to pass on a bright and balmy Southern California spring day that I made my intentions known, warning the boys that if I did not receive one outstanding lead out of the thirty-one guys, they all would spend their vacation in summer school. I placed the deadline for submissions to the following Monday, giving the little bastards the weekend to come up with something acceptable, little realizing that the assignment would unleash one pent-up emotion, a lead that became famous in the annals of St. Augustine High School.

On Monday, I greeted a very subdued group of lads at my classroom's door. Missing was the noise, the adolescent prattle usually assaulting my ears of a Monday morn; the lads filed silently into the room, quickly taking their assigned seats. I stood in awe of their metamorphosed deportment. Perhaps, I thought, they had prayed for guidance or a miracle to Saint Jude, the "Saint of Impossible Cases" and felt secure in the knowledge that through the intercession of Jude, a satisfying lead would be submitted, a topic sentence to bail out their sorry keisters.

Roll taken and in a voice that would have filled Stentor, the loudmouthed Greek herald, with envy, I directed each row to pass forward their papers. As I collected the thirty-odd papers, peace reigned throughout the class. Then, retiring ceremoniously behind my desk, I began scanning through the stack of papers, the class's eyes riveted on my fingers peeling back page after page.

After purposely extending the search, I plucked one paper from the pile, and holding it like a proud bird hunter showing off his newly downed pheasant, I loudly exclaimed, "This is it! Gentlemen, I have my perfect lead, a sentence that promises a superior paper, a paper screaming to be read, a paper, I reckon, that will result in my granting its author an 'A' and granting the rest of you clemency." I felt like San Quentin's warden granting a condemned man a stay of execution.

Holding up the paper for all to see, I felt like secretary of war, Henry Stimson, drawing the card of the first Selective Service draftee in 1940. How I loved my autonomy! Holding the paper at arm's length like a herald in a Shakespearean play, I slowly announced the name of the class's savior, "Tom Graciano." All eyes shifted to Graciano's desk where he sat grinning like an escapee from a mental institution.

"And, gentlemen, here's Tom's perfect lead, '*Mr. Bowman is full of shit.*'"

The sentence became legend, quoted at class reunions, over drinks at the class's annual post-Christmas get-together, and bringing down the house at my retirement bash in 1993, a party attended by friends, former students, a college professor, and my parish priest, who, when hearing the story recounted to the gathering by its originator, laughed so hard he damned near fell off his chair. Although the remark left some attendees aghast, most thought it was a hoot; a few marveled at my magnanimity in not having killed Graciano. Some years later, I was apprised that it had been Graciano's father who had given his son the idea. The old man knew me "when," and it was he who planted the seed that led to the blooming of "the perfect sentence."

YEAR OF DECISION

$\mathcal{I}$n the spring of 1977, my sixteenth year on the teaching staff of St. Augustine High School, I was faced with a career-changing decision: The previous year I had turned fifty ("half a century" in the words of my eldest child), and except for Social Security, I had accrued not a farthing toward my retirement at age sixty-five. What to do? Although I had acquired a state of California Teaching Credential, making me eligible to teach language arts in the public school system, there was a problem: None of the school districts, including the community college, was hiring. It isn't that I was tired of teaching at an all-boys' Catholic high school, but more a case of worrying about my future, about my "pipe-and-slippers" days that lay just around the corner. I was, in a word, desperate. I began sending letters to old acquaintances who were teachers and/or coaches, or both, hoping that one of them could provide me with at least an interview with their principal or superintendent; a month went by without so much as a "there may be a possibility." The lyrics of a song popularized by its inclusion in a sappy World-War-II movie summed up my situation, "The pickings are poor and the crop is lean." Then, when I had all but given up hope of landing a position, I received a telephone call from a most unlikely source.

I did not recognize the voice on the other end of the line. "Don't you recognize the voice, John?" My first thought was—a bill collector; then, perhaps it was a boyhood chum.

"John, it's Mike, Mike Cunningham."

The only Cunningham I could recall was a kid we expelled for passing out condoms to practically the entire junior class.

"Are you the rubber supplier we booted a few years back?" I asked.

"What the hell are you talking about? I'm the coach whose freshman football team kicked the shit out of your frosh team last season! Good God!

I have known you since I was twelve and playing in the La Mesa *Pony* League.

I'm a Saints' alum, class of 1959!"

Suddenly, it dawned on me.

"Geez, Mike, I'm really sorry for not having recognized you. I hope you will excuse my ignorance. What can I do for you?"

"No, John, I think it's what I can do for you."

I didn't know where all this was heading, but I was curious and asked what he was driving at. "Are you interested in a teaching position?" Is a boy interested in apple pie?

"Where," I blurted?

Mike continued, "I am the varsity football coach at Ramona High School, and I need a frosh football coach who can also teach English and assume the duties of advisor to the student body council."

"When do I start?" I blurted.

"Whoa, not so fast, amigo," he cautioned. "You've first got to be interviewed by our principal, Mr. Bill, and I have arranged for the two of you to meet each other at four next Wednesday afternoon. Be there!"

I was there, and five minutes early. Enter Myron Bill, "stage right!"

"So, Mr. Bowman, you're interested in joining our faculty?" the blue-suit sitting across the desk from me asked, his remark conjuring remembrances of sixteen years past when the same question was asked by a priest. God, I thought, I hope this offer doesn't come with a salary of $4,000 a year!

"Well," he continued. "Mike informs me that you are highly thought of as a teacher of English at St. Augustine High School. Do you feel you can teach our country kids to write?" Looking Mr. Bill straight in the eye, I brazenly replied, "Mr. Bill, I think I have the skills to teach a rock to write."

Needless to say, my remark left Mr. Bill vexed. For a moment, he sat, staring at me, seemingly attempting to decide whether to applaud my remark, have me committed to the loony bin, or kick my ass out of his office; finally, regaining his composure, adjusting his necktie, and repositioning his eyeglasses, he leaned his elbows on his desk and muttered, "We'll be in touch."

He said he was glad to have met me and wished me a good day. I thought I had screwed up, blown my chances of being hired. I should have heeded Mike's advice, "John, I want to caution you about your interview with Mr. Bill. He is not a complicated person. He hails from North Dakota, and talking to him is like talking to Lawrence Welk." (That remark told me all I needed to know.) Now I was sure I wouldn't be hired: a'wunnerful, a'wunnerful. So, at the end of the spring semester, I informed Fr. K that I would be returning in the fall, but change lay just around the corner.

With the school year ended, I wasted no time in packing my trailer and station wagon, and with son Conway riding shotgun, pointing the Chrysler north to begin our fourth annual trip to Central Idaho and Redfish Lake, where the two of us would spend another glorious summer, fly-fishing, and, in my case, working as the lodge's fishing guide. Conway? He would resume his annual Huckleberry Finn lifestyle for the ensuing two months, meaning he would fish, kayak, operate his fish-cleaning business, and bath only after someone threw him in the lake, hence his nickname, "Dirtman." Needless to say, he was the envy of all his chums who spent their summer vacation swimming in La Mesa's Municipal pool or skateboarding the sidewalks.

Then, a few weeks after settling into our idyllic routine, I received a phone call from my wife advising me that I was scheduled for an interview in Ramona the sixth of July; I quickly phoned Delta Airlines, reserving a seat on the next flight to San Diego. Then farming out the care of Conway to some friends, I packed a small bag, and the next morning kissed Conway good-bye, pointed the Chrysler's nose south toward Twin Falls, and on my way home, my prospects for a new employment seemingly within my reach; as it turned out, I was hired, signed a contract, and broke the news to Fr. Keane, who was most understanding. "John, I wish you well, and although I hate to see you leave, I fully understand your reasons for leaving. I only wish we could offer our faculty a good retirement plan, but finances as they stand really makes it impossible."

I told him that I understood, thanked him for the support he had afforded me over the years, and stated that when I retired from the public school system, I hoped he would welcome me back as a substitute. I left campus with mixed emotions, overjoyed to be at long last working in a venue that offered security in the so-called golden years older years; saddened to taking leave of a school allowed me the freedom to truly teach to my strengths and not be encumbered by the pedagogical claptrap spawned by addlepated professors who never taught English to a classroom full of horny, pimple-faced lads; however, in a few weeks, I discovered much to my dismay that the new school district was intolerant of the teacher who thumbed his nose at the established curriculum.

My first two years on the teaching staff at Ramona High were a living hell, an environment so unrewarding that I began giving seriously thought to returning to SAHS if they would have me; for instance, about my third week I was confronted by the mother of a young man I had in my sophomore English class. The mother and I met in the counselor's office for a discussion concerning the boy's class assignments. The kid lived on a local hog ranch and used to come into class smelling like pig shit, his boots covered with the stuff; if that wasn't bad enough, he seldom came prepared for class discussion, the real reason for the conference. I did, however plan to broach the problem of the boy's bringing the noxious stench into the classroom. The conference began, and, like the 101st Airborne at Bastogne in 1944, I was suddenly on the defensive; the mother came at me with the speed of Hitler's panzers! "What in the name of all that is holy are you trying to teach my son? He doesn't need to study literature or English grammar to read the directions on a feedbag!"

VI

The 1980s, 1990s, and 2000s

SORRY, BRIGHAM YOUNG

*T*he comely young lady stood, requesting that the gathering at table push aside their dessert plates and give her their undivided attention; to me, her former high school English teacher, she respectfully invited me to "keep my mouth shut" and pay rapt attention to what she was about to impart. I did. She then announced she had something to say regarding my spiritual well-being; however, before getting to the gist of this episode, I think, perhaps, I should, in the words of Maria von Trapp, "start at the very beginning."

In the 1980s, I was teaching a full load at Ramona High School in San Diego's North County. Ramona is a quaint rural community that was, at one time, referred to as the Turkey Capitol of the United States. As a child, I recall my grandfather loading our entire family into his 1934 DeSoto sedan and heading for The Valley of the Sun, another area sobriquet. Although we could just as easily have purchased our Thanksgiving bird from either one of the two butcher shops in our town, grandfather insisted we motor thirty-plus arduous miles over partially paved roads, risking flat tires and overheated radiators, to purchase what today is termed a "free-range" gobbler. To me, a seven-year-old, a drumstick was a drumstick, free-range or no free-range, but as usual, the old presbyter had his way. But less I digress too much, let me return to Ramona High School of the 1980s.

Ramona High School was not a college-prep institution. Most of the youngsters were kids right off the farm, where raising poultry or slopping hogs constituted their world; few desired a college education. Some few had a difficult time receiving a high school diploma. Good kids? Yes, when a mother announced that studying literature a waste of time because all she wanted her children to learn was how to read the instruction manual for a milking machine. "Did that Charlie Dickens ever pull a teat?" There were, thank God, exceptions.

One family in particular produced a bevy of youngsters who not only understood the milking machine manual but were also talented enough to have written the instructional book, teenagers who, through their parents' encouragement, began high school fully acquainted with the works of the world's great authors: Homer, Dickens, Twain, Austen, the Bronte sisters, and a host of other classical writers; the first young lady I had the good fortune to enter in my roll book had read Austen's *Pride and Prejudice* before she was a sophomore. She couldn't milk a cow, but she could discuss in great detail and with critical insight Elizabeth's prejudice and Darcy's pride, plus the scatterbrained and garrulous Mrs. Bennet and the witty cynicism of mild-mannered Mr. Bennet. A member of the Church of Latter Day Saints, she excelled also as a dogged recruiter for her faith. And while a member of my class during her junior and senior years, she took on the task of inducing me to become a follower of Joseph Smith, founder of the LDS. But let's return to the gathering.

"Mr. Bowman, my siblings and I have invited you to this restaurant not only to join us in dinner but to make an announcement."

Reaching into her purse, she drew out a small, gift-wrapped, diagonal box, and holding the box up for all to see, then looking me straight in the eye she said, "For more semesters than we, my sisters, brother, and I care to recount, you have continually made life almost unbearable with your constant ranting about preferring the fountain pen to the ballpoint. Therefore, we have all contributed coin of the realm for the purchase of this Italian manufactured fountain pen upon which we have taken the liberty of having your name engraved on its clip. We hope you will like it. It comes to you with all our love and appreciation for the wonderful teaching not only of literature and composition but also the manner in which you have shared with us your life experiences and your spiritual beliefs. In an effort to induce you to become a member the Church of Latter Day Saints, we have worked feverishly in our efforts to convert you. However, we have failed, not because of lackluster effort, but because of your deep devotion to the Roman Catholic Church, something we all greatly admire."

Then giving me a smile and a wink, she announced that it had been determined that I could remain a Catholic.

I have the pen to this day and am still attending seven o'clock Mass every Sunday. When it's time for the Prayers of the Faithful, with the prayers to all the members of my immediate family, I include the names of all those lovely youngsters with whom I am in contact to this day.

CALLING MR. SEMICOLON

I had not been feeling well for the better part of three years, but like most men, I was unwilling to visit our family doctor for fear that he would tell me I had an incurable disease and but a few months to live. So I continued teaching, my gut hurting so much that on some days, I barely managed to make it until the final bell. Rather than consulting my doctor friends, I began diagnosing myself, surmising that the attacks of acid indigestion were triggered by a habit, cultivated in the military, of not masticating enough the overloads of food I ingested; my abdominal pains were the price I paid for my weekly grading sessions of gut-wrenching stacks of syntactical pratfalls. Besides, I reckoned, my weekly sessions with the "Dr. Kildare" TV series more than qualified me as a medical expert. In any event, the problem came to a head three nights following my sixty-seventh-birthday, as I lay in bed, my entire body contorted by excruciating pains.

Earlier that day, I began feeling a slight pressure in my abdomen accompanied by nauseous, painful spasms. I deduced that the problem was the result of the lamb-chops eaten the previous evening. As day gave way to evening, the pains became more and more excruciating, so much so that my son, Conway, insisted he drive me to the local hospital. Practically doubled over in pain, it took little encouragement for me to acquiesce. An hour later found me wrapped in a hospital gown, my bare bum protruding from the gown's open end, undergoing an EKG, an x-ray, and blood and urine tests; sedated, wheeled into a holding room, and covered by a warm blanket, I drifted into a drug-induced doze, awakened later by someone moving around in my ER cubicle.

It proved the ER doctor, who, having positioned my x-ray on the viewing screen, ran his hand in a semicircle across the shadowed picture of my intestines muttering, "J . . . e . . . e . . . sus Christ!"

I knew I was in trouble. Five hours later found me lying on an operating table; six hours later found me lying in bed, my body sprouting tubes of many dimensions, my abdomen stapled shut, my legs encased in two pulsating plastic sleeves applied to reduce my chances of developing blood clots; oh, I almost forgot, there was a catheter approximately three feet long sticking out the end of my Johnson, traversing my leg into a bag, plus a colostomy bag glued onto my exposed intestine. I felt like Dr. Frankenstein's monster.

During my five-day hospital stay, I was visited by family, friends, and (Are you ready for this?) students by the score who brought things I couldn't eat but food that the nurses and aides consumed with great relish. Cards, notes, and stuffed animals bedecked my room. But the topper of my stay occurred one evening as I shifted my body, attempting to find a comfortable sleeping position, when the phone rang. It was one of my high school students.

He had heard that I was hospitalized and was calling to find out how I was, his American history teacher having advised him of my surgery . . . He seemed relieved, after I had belied his fear that I might be ready for the coroner, I assuring him I was doing well and about to be discharged from the hospital in a few days.

Then, in an interested tone, he asked, "Is it true, sir, the surgeon removed twenty-eight inches of your colon?" Yes, it was true.

"Gee, sir, that's a tad more than nine yards!" It was, I agreed.

"Well, Mr. Bowman," he quipped. "May we call you Mr. Semicolon?"

Convulsed in laughter, my staples about to pop out, I was forced to hang up; ever the teacher, I wondered if the youngster had been listening during my lectures on punctuation and had specifically paid attention during the segment on the proper use of the semicolon. I was happy he hadn't the knowledge of my being obliged to wear a colostomy bag because he might have asked, "May we refer to you as Mr. Gasbag?" Oh, how wickedly delightful is the mind of the adolescent!

MAC, IRVING, AND GEORGE: MY THREE ANGELS

*W*hen I hear some shameless galoot announce that he's a "self-made man," I cringe. There is no such thing; we all owe much of what we have achieved in life to many of the individuals who have positively influenced us on our journey through life, whether it be parent, friend, teacher, or, in the case of many Catholic-educated men, to the hard-nosed nun, armed with the everready-to-smack-you-over-the-knuckles ruler, whose sole purpose in life was to educate you not only academically, but spiritually as well.

In my case, I owe much of my success to three men met at different stages of my life, men who, sensing my potential, helped free me from a fen of failure where I had been mired most of my life. They were the angels on my shoulder 'who through persistence and patience helped me take the first steps to a better, more fulfilling, life. To each of them, I am eternally grateful; all of them passed away within two years of each other, but until I, too, shake off this mortal coil, each man will be enshrined in my mind, for without them, I would be mired still in that bog of shortcomings.

I have, in previous chapters, dealt with how each man shaped my life, acknowledging where I would be today had it not been for their TLC. Borrowing from the writings of Saint Ambrose who advised Man "to pray to the angels, for they are given to us as guardians." To that I say Amen! I was blessed with three angels.

Postscript: 7 September 2009. Today, in the company of a former student and dear a friend, I attended "A Celebration of Life" affair honoring Dr. George C. Gross, who "Crossed the Bar" a few weeks past. Teaching associates, former students, and one university administrator apprised a large gathering of the role Dr. Gross had played in their lives, as educator and friend. As the Brits are wont to say, all the speakers were "spot on." A member of the so-called "greatest generation," George Gross was a gentleman, a private man, a man not given to self-promotion, a man who, as a citizen soldier, served his country honorably during World War II, a humble and gracious individual who never flaunted his accomplishments, either as a sergeant in an armored unit, or as a scholar who for decades inspired high school and college students of every bent to love the written word, the poetry of John Keats and Geoffrey Chaucer, perhaps the most important English writer of the 14th century; it was through the works of these two poets, and especially in the works of Chaucer, that George became a high-school teaching legend, able to enthrall his seniors with Chaucer's masterpiece, "The Canterbury Tales," no small accomplishment when presenting the work to a classroom full of 17-and-18-year olds; but I knew another side of George that I admired: He was a wise and caring person, a man whose like I may never see again. Requiescat in pace, George.

DEAR MR. BOWMAN . . .
A TREASURE TROVE OF MEMORIES

Dear Mr. Bowman,

We would like to express our appreciation to you for the progress achieved by our son, Karl, this year in your English class. Yours has been a class that Karl has been looking forward to every day. Not only have you challenged and motivated the youngster, you have managed to work on some of his very human traits that are better done without. Very few teachers seem to find the time and inclination to devote the personal attention to all of the student's educationally related character development needs.

Thank you for being the teacher with insight, flair, and dedication that all caring parents hope their children will experience.

Respectfully yours,
(A concerned parent)

1981

This note was the result of my having physically removed this woman's son from my GATE class, a program offered by the school district to outstanding junior high school eighth graders in which the youngsters were instructed in high school subjects, the classes meeting, following the end of the official school day on the high school campus. The young man and six of his classmates formed the initial group placed into my English class; all of the youngsters, and especially the young man in question, learned lessons not listed in the class's syllabus.

It was a Tuesday afternoon when this program began. I was a bit perplexed having never taught students in this age-group. Would they accept a teacher who early in his career had been christened JBT—John Bowman Tyrant—by his students? But, more importantly, would their parents approve of my drill instructor discipline? My unorthodox teaching methods? My stinginess in the awarding of grades? My unwillingness to accept base work? A curriculum which emphasized writing in its varying forms? A few of my questions were about to be answered as seven prattling teens entered my classroom, my "please be seated ladies and gentlemen" drawing nothing but contemptuous sneers from the seven bodies frozen in the doorway.

Enter JBT, stage left. "Are you all deaf? I said sit down, and I mean now, not tomorrow!" The two girls walked to their desks with stiff dignity; the boys, seemingly annoyed, shrugged their shoulders in mock resignation and slithered their fourteen-year-old frames into desks. From behind my lectern, I gave the once-over to the row in which the students were sitting, the boys, save for one young man braced like a West Point cadet, contorted in shapes that made my back ache. Removing myself from behind my lectern, I proceeded to wend my way up the aisle while at the same time explaining what would be expected of them during the weeks they were under my tutelage. "The purpose of this class is to teach writing. We learn writing in three ways: by studying grammar, sentence structure, mechanics, and organization, by studying the writing of professional writers, and by practicing in those writing skills you have already learned. I will provide you with many different types of good prose to examine and to use as models and suggest many topics for you to write about."

Returning to the protection of my lectern, I continued, "I will accept nothing but best efforts in all exercises and assignments. Anything less will result in a failing grade."

Pushing my horn-rims to the end of my nose, I asked, "Are there any questions?" Out of the corner of my left eye, I spied a raised hand; it was the ersatz cadet, his dress more in keeping with an Ivy Leaguer. He wore well-pressed chinos, blue oxford-cloth shirt, penny loafers, and argyle socks. He was a handsome kid, clean-cut, with nary a hair out of place on his perfectly formed pate. But despite his good grooming, I sensed something in his demeanor that spelled trouble, and my hunch wasn't wrong.

"Question, sir?"

With a voice both resonant and impressive, but one tinged with a small amount of annoyance, he asked, "You don't expect us to meet all of your demands, do you?"

I retorted that I did, and he, in particular, would.

"Well, then, Mr. whatever-your-name is, what if I refuse?"

Directing one of the other boys to open the classroom door, I reached out, grabbed the collar of his shirt, and yanked him out of his desk, dragged him to the open door, thrusting him into hallway where he landed on his khaki-encased ass! Slamming the door, I returned to my lectern. "Now," I asked. "Are there any more questions?"

The young ladies, their mouths spread into thin-lipped smiles, sat primly; the boys, their bodies uncontorted, sat upright, eyes fixed on me. Attentive silence! Teacher one, students zero, while outside the classroom a muffled voice, like a broken record, kept repeating, "You'll hear from my mother, mister!" And the boy proved a prophet.

The next day as I regaled my junior American literature class with my insights into the use of understatement by Ernest Miller Hemingway, there was a knock at my classroom door. "Enter," I yelled, angered by the interruption to my insightful lecture. The door opened, and in walked the most handsome (not beautiful) woman I had ever set eyes upon. In an Eastern European accent laced with the richness found in a plate of *galumpkis* (Polish cabbage balls), the lady asked if I "vas dot teacher dat trew my sown out uf da class." I replied I was. "Vy?" Not desiring my class to be witness to what might well prove an ugly confrontation between a teacher and an irate parent, I requested they begin reading Hemingway's short story, "Indian Camp."

Then opening the door, I ushered her outside; once out of earshot, we talked, and talked, and talked, the gist of our conversation dealing with young Carl, a lad, according to his mother, who "vas too bick fur hees breetches!" I pointed out to the lady that in light of my having known her boy but a few days, I was in no position to pass judgment on him. She thanked me for my honesty, a trait she said she found lacking in some of her boy's teachers. Then, breaking into an open, friendly smile requested that I take her boy in hand, physically if necessary, assuring me that I had her permission to do whatever I thought pertinent to the situation, then thanking me, she turned, and with a springy bounce, strode down the hall, leaving me in an euphoric state, delighted that I had finally met a parent who didn't want me run out of town for having disciplined her darling.

The kid was back in my class next day, the picture of social decorum; eight years later, he was in the commencement line at Stanford University. My "power-of-suggestion" tactics must have impressed him, because there is no record either in high school or in Palo Alto of his having pulled the smart shit he pulled on me when he was fourteen. John Dewey, the father of American progressive education, would have frowned on my methods which were more de Sade than Dewey.

Carl's mom? She was described as a dedicated citizen whose leadership and devotion to improving the quality of education in the town of Ramona exemplified the thought that "the world is upheld by children who study."(Paraphrasing The Talmud)

The wonderful lady cast off the coil too early, passing away only months before her fiftieth birthday. A handsome woman of commanding presence, when she spoke you listened, her voice impressive and compassionate. She was the most delightful parent with whom I had dealings during my thirty-six years as a high school instructor. I shall never forget her. Carl? Happily married, the father of three precocious children, a success, and, I might add, one of my special friends, a man who to this day refers to me as his uncle John.

I have been away from this machine for the better part of a month, my mind in a state of inertia, my mind immobile, bereft of the ideas that have sustained me these many years as I have labored composing this owning-up. Last evening, however, my attendance at a high school reunion provided me a fertile field of ideas.

The St. Augustine High School class of 1968 gathered at the all-boys' school for their fortieth reunion; it's the custom of the alumni of this Catholic school to invite special teachers to join them in the evening's festivities that include a Mass in the school's chapel, a social hour in the school's patio, and a superb supper funded by the alumni association. There is provided ample time for mending a few fences erected many years past, the opportunity to heal wounds, physical as well a psychological. But more importantly, it's a time that lends proof to our having been a community despite our being on opposite sides of the desk or speaker's podium.

To the teachers assembled, the fifty-eight-year-old men were our students still, we their mentors. Though many of us had undergone changes—graying hair, bald pates, furrowed faces, corpulent girths, and matronly helpmates—one characteristic remained unchanged: our deep respect for each other. Oh, hell, yes, we managed with wisecracks and flippancy to conceal our true feelings, but love shone in our eyes. Though age had taken its toll, I pictured them still as the bright-eyed, smart-assed kids I had crossed verbal swords with so many years past, remaining in my mind the all-knowing teens I had nurtured in the 1960s, and now, having cast off the pale of adolescence, had returned as authors, publishers, educators, bankers, therapists, stock brokers, real estate agents, public servants, and one guy, the pitchman for a local cemetery. ("Mr. Bowman, I can get plots for you and Mrs. Bowman at a discount.") I don't know who was prouder, they or I. And now, sitting at my laptop, puffing on my favorite briar, I sense a certain pride in having been a positive factor in these young men, and not only those at this particular gathering but on the hundreds of young people, girls and boys, who studied under my tutelage, whose parents entrusted their youngsters' lives into my care.

Some years past, five other instructors and I were being considered for the teacher of the year award. The principal decided that a group of juniors and seniors who had attended the school for at least three years should select "a teacher they most respected and felt had contributed significantly to their education." Modesty aside, I was their unanimous choice. My selection, I believe, is best summed up in the words of the school's principal, "John Bowman is perhaps the most demanding teacher I know. He demands quantity but especially quality. Students are motivated to truly do their best work. Frequently I hear students express surprised pride in their work for Mr. Bowman's class. No student 'gets by with shoddy work or incompletes.' Your best is expected on all work. Attending or watching a John Bowman class is an exciting, stimulating experience. It is both challenging and entertaining. Marshall McLuhan once wrote, 'That which pleases teaches best.' John Bowman 'does that' better than anyone I have observed. The rich background and constant references to a variety of sources, experiences, and ideas keep students engaged in the class. The delivery is exciting and uplifting, requiring active listening and demanding participation. There are no lulls or passive moments in a Bowman class. Whenever I visit Mr. Bowman's class, I understand why he was chosen to be honored as 'Teacher of the Year.' His lectures and discussions are so intriguing I am always tempted to sit and get involved."

Principal Ramona High School
1989

I received the following message from a foreign exchange student, presently a visiting scholar at MIT:

> I have known John Bowman for more than twenty years and have cherished every single moment of his friendship, guidance, and support. Trying to summarize in just a few words what John has meant to me, and to so many students before and after me, is almost impossible. His drive, pastoral care, and unflinching determination in improving his students, both in academic and personal lives, is invaluable. At times, he can be challenging and demanding but so is life, and being able to learn early that what is important, comes at a "price," is very valuable. I am amazed when I find myself teaching my students the lessons I have learned from John.
>
> Cambridge, June 25, 2008.

From the pen of another student, a high school teacher for more than thirty years, I received the following:

> My third year I faced the terrors inflicted by John Bowman, my senior English teacher. During my junior year I had been in a class next door to his, and I and my classmates frequently heard pounding, yelling, and then laughter coming from the class. We were terrified! All we could imagine was that someone in his class had said something stupid and had been thrown up against the wall to be ridiculed by the entire class. We, my classmates, and I entered his room, already cowed by the legend and his fierce reputation, the knowledge that he did not suffer fools and that he did not spare criticism.
>
> To our relief, we quickly discovered that the pounding came from Mr. Bowman slamming his open hand on his desk top for emphasis, as frequently in praise of a good comment as in disgust for one that displeased him. Our written work was treated with contempt for much of the first quarter, but we quickly learned how to write and how to please the great man. There was no better day, no greater compliment, than the moment he called on me and I ventured an answer to a question he had posed and he slammed his hand on his desk with satisfaction. "Mr. Waldron!" he shouted. "Say that again!"
>
> It took most of the year to figure out how much he loved his class. We knew he loved literature—Sophocles, Shakespeare, Thoreau, Steinbeck, and Ernest Hemingway—all of them were literary heroes. However, he was also a consummate actor, able to hide his affection for us as long as he could. By year's end, when he handed out his homemade awards for excellence, we were allies with him and his secret. The incoming juniors would never know. But I knew. And I wanted to be like him.
>
> Though I could never "be like him," I managed to learn some of my key values from him—passion, humor, a dedication to excellence, and a commitment to making every student feel included, honored, respected. I'd like to think that my mentor would be proud.

(This young man was nominated as a candidate for the San Diego County teacher of the year; the above was taken from his professional biography, a copy which he forwarded to me.) Not caring to run the risk of being branded a male chauvinist, I think it only proper that I include praise received from the distaff side. This paean was from a young lady I taught during the 1979-80 school year:

I was in your freshman English class in late 1970s. We had a very rocky start. On the first day of class, you stated that anyone who didn't want to work very, very hard should see you after class and get out of your class. Being a basically lazy person, as I feel we all are, I came to you after class and tried to get out. You wouldn't let me, and I was angry with you for months! By the time the year was over, I realized how much you had helped me and had not only thanked you for not letting me drop your class but was part of a committee attempting to get the school to assign you a sophomore English class for the next school year. Unfortunately, we were unsuccessful, resulting in my never having the privilege of having you as a teacher again.

I feel very nervous writing this. I almost expect it to be returned with red-penned "awks") written all over it. However, I think of you often and with great fondness and respect. My years at RHS were very difficult, and in my opinion, then and now, largely a waste of time. I eventually wound up skipping my senior year to take the CHSPE and begin community college at sixteen. However, although it took me a few years to realize it, what I learned from you during that one year was enough.

You have helped me in ways I never dreamed possible. All through college, my professors, without exception, remarked that my writing skills were above average, and yours was the only composition class I had ever taken. I have been a legal secretary for almost six years, and the reason I am valued in this field is my writing ability, as well as my knowledge of grammar, etc.

Although I never imagined myself writing to you, I recently unearthed a quotation in one of my favorite readings . . . teaching high school students is like dropping stones down a well and listening for the splash, only most of the time you never hear it . . . As a teacher, the only reward or acknowledgment I can ever receive that really means anything is to hear from one of you that something I taught you or caused you to realize has actually made a difference in your life." I don't know if you feel this way, but I thought I would drop you this note anyway to thank you once again for refusing to let me drop your class.

I hope you and your family are well. God bless you.

Sincerely,

May 26, 1994.

With sugar there has to be a little vinegar, and the following "fan" letter, the antithesis of the billets-doux, I received from a lad with whom I had had numerous differences of opinion:

> I imagine you are receiving all sorts of praise from the class's toadies about how you taught them so much. Well, mister, you won't get that shit from me. Though you seemed to know your subject, I found your class a real pain in the ass. All your bullshit stories about your youth were the most boring crap I have ever heard. I am happy I am leaving this school and leaving you. My mother was right when she said that you were wasting our time studying Inglish (sic) literature. I really failed to see the importance of your reading Chaucer in Middle Inglish (sic). What do I care about the many husbands of the wife of bath (sic). I pity the kids coming into your class next semester. Good-bye and as my mom says, "Good riddance of bad garbage."

> Senior
> Class of 1984

Author's note: And I so liked his mother.

PS: Yesterday noon, over steaming plates of Mexican burritos, a former student and I discussed, between large gulps of ice tea (The burritos were *muy caliente*), what each of us regarded as the most compensatory of all the rewards of teaching. The young man has taught high school for past twenty-five years, and quite successfully, I might add. Anyway, we both agreed that the money in itself was important; however, there was one recompense not measured in dollars or cents, and that was how many of our former students honored us with letters, notes, and cards of all kinds. It made us feel good to be remembered, to learn that we are not forgotten, that most of the youngsters we taught think enough of us to take the time to thank us for not only teaching them a subject but also for taking the time to understand them, in many cases, better than their parents.

Our lunch finished, we left the restaurant. Standing outside on the sidewalk, we made small talk for a few minutes before departing, promising to keep in touch with each other; he requested that I visit his classroom as I had in years past and discuss with his students Hemingway's short stories. The kids never failed to write, thanking me for having shared with them. Following my first visit to the school in 2005, my habit of opening a class with a single question related to the works assigned in preparation for my visit, drew a response from a young lady who said she was amazed that I would open a class as I did, and she wanted to know why as none of her other teachers practiced that technique. In reply to her question, I said I did so to not only determine if the short stories had been read, but, more importantly, how deeply they had been read and also as a means of proving to her and her classmates that they were capable of grasping the meaning in even the most complex of stories, poems, or plays.

During my many years in the classroom, I challenged students to reach for answers to the things they didn't know; for instance, "Why are Nick Adams's physical actions so methodical in Ernest Hemingway's 'The Big Two-Hearted River?'" This practice made for some very interesting classes, while putting to rest the sacrosanct idea held by many instructors that "smarts" are limited to adults!

PS: Never in my thirty-eight years in the classroom did I ever feel that I had chosen the wrong profession. I contend that teaching is not just a job; it's a calling.

Max: You've Been a Long Time Coming Lad

---

*Y*esterday as I walked you to sleep while you lay in my arms, I realized just how happy you have made me, young man. It had been forty-four years since I held your father in my arms while I paced the floor, crooning to the little guy, a chap you closely resemble. You have been born to your wonderful mother and dad and into two loving families of grandparents, aunts, and uncles. I know not how many years I have left on this earth, but your coming has triggered in me a desire to remain for a few more years in which I can love you, take you to football games, teach you to fish, read to you, and be the loving grandfather you deserve. But just in case I am unable to assist you in these goals, I want you to know how very much I love you. Your birth is the sixth happy occasion afforded me in my eighty-six years on this planet, the first was marrying your grandmother, the remaining four the birth of your dad and your three aunts.

Much Love, Gramps

A FINAL WORD

*H*ow can I close out something that has been a part of my life, a partial compilation of my life that began in earnest in the early years of my thirty-eight-year teaching career, a memoir that I have promised to self-publish since early 2000, a work that many of my former students are dying to read, an American success story that verily shouts, "This guy's life is an American success story?" Certainly, it does not match the financial successes of Andrew Carnegie, John D. Rockefeller, or Henry Ford. What it concerns is the life of a high school dropout who became a successful high school teacher, a guy who never earned more than $42, 000 a year, a lout who for years was mired in a fen of failure, a man who lent credence to the notion that "God works in strange and mysterious ways."

I began thinking about writing this work of love when I was thirty-three years old; in a few months, the Lord willing, I turn eighty-four. During that period of time, I've been blessed with four wonderful children who are my pride and joy, remained married to my lovely Irish wife; taught thousands of America's youngsters, many my dear friends to this day; hunted and fished with some of God's greatest creations, and taught in the company of more than a few dedicated teachers; anything I have omitted you'll find on the pages of this book. In some instances, I may have embellished a bit, airbrushed a tad;however, the experiences are true, many bittersweet in their subject matter, some tragic, but most of the matter contributed to my development from a scalawag to a responsible human being. Oh, I am not so smug as to think that I am without faults. A philosopher once stated that "Man falls at least seven times a day," and I am no exception. I am at this stage of my life, satisfied that when my time comes to "cast of this mortal coil," I will leave with a clear conscience, knowing in my heart that, with the help of the Almighty, I have served mankind as best I could.

AFTERWORD

$\mathcal{D}$ear reader: My plan initially was to divide into chapters this recounting of my life; however, what I have written lends better itself to labeling as vignettes my life's experiences, sketches loosely categorized and arranged within the decades in which they happened, resulting in some pieces set in overlapping years, for instance, 1930s-40s. Also I wish you to consider as you read how many years have passed since my birth in 1926. The passing of years tends to muddle the mind when recounting events of many years past; therefore, I beg your indulgence if I sometimes tend to embellish the truth. It's a human failing, but a fault we all share.

You need but listen to your grandfather's retelling of his experiences in World War II. Although a crewman in the United States Army Air Force, his combat experience was limited to depositing lots of fifty caliber lead into the Gulf of Mexico while undergoing training in a Combat Unit school. Truth be known, when he arrived in the U.K. in April of '45, his Group was on "stand-down," resulting in his never flying one combat mission. But to hear old Grandpa tell it, he was credited with downing five Me 109s. He did, however, look "smashing" in his uniform and gunner's wings.

As you forgive Grandpa for his verbal ornamentations, I ask that you accord me the same respect; after all, I am eighty-five, a Grandpa, and a WWII Army Air Force vet.

Peace!

Edwards Brothers Malloy
Thorofare, NJ USA
March 24, 2014